W9-DCB-829

THE BRILLIANCE
OF BLACK BOYS

THE BRILLIANCE OF BLACK BOYS

CULTIVATING SCHOOL SUCCESS IN THE EARLY GRADES

BRIAN L. WRIGHT
WITH SHELLY L. COUNSELL

Foreword by James Earl Davis

TEACHERS COLLEGE PRESS

TEACHERS COLLEGE | COLUMBIA UNIVERSITY
NEW YORK AND LONDON

Published by Teachers College Press, 1234 Amsterdam Avenue, New York, NY 10027

Copyright © 2018 by Teachers College, Columbia University

Cover design by Holly Grundon Design. Cover photo of local Memphis schoolchildren courtesy of Porter-Leath.

Chapter 5 contains figures adapted from *Roots and Wings: Affirming Culture and Preventing Bias in Early Childhood Education* (3rd ed.), by Stacey York, 2016, St Paul, MN: Redleaf Press. Reprinted with permission of Redleaf Press, www.redleaf.org.

Chapter 5 contains a figure from Anti-Bias Education for Young Children and Ourselves, by L. Derman-Sparks & J. Olsen Edwards, 2010, Washington, DC. NAEYC. Copyright © 2010 NAEYC. Reprinted with permission.

All rights reserved. No part of this publication may be reproduced or transmitted in any form or by any means, electronic or mechanical, including photocopy, or any information storage and retrieval system, without permission from the publisher. For reprint permission and other subsidiary rights requests, please contact Teachers College Press, Rights Dept.: tcpressrights@tc.columbia.edu

Library of Congress Cataloging-in-Publication Data

Names: Wright, Brian L., author. | Counsell, Shelly, author.
Title: The brilliance of Black boys : cultivating school success in the early grades / Brian L. Wright with Shelly Counsell.
Description: New York, NY : Teachers College Press, [2018] | Includes bibliographical references and index.
Identifiers: LCCN 2017053028 (print) | LCCN 2018005220 (ebook) | ISBN 9780807776810 (ebook) | ISBN 9780807758922 (pbk. : alk. paper)
Subjects: LCSH: African Americans—Education (Early childhood) | African American boys—Education—Social aspects.
Classification: LCC LC2765 (ebook) | LCC LC2765 .W75 2018 (print) | DDC 371.829/96073—dc23
LC record available at https://lccn.loc.gov/2017053028

ISBN 978-0-8077-5892-2 (paper)
ISBN 978-0-8077-7681-0 (ebook)

Printed on acid-free paper
Manufactured in the United States of America

25 24 23 22 21 20 19 18   8 7 6 5 4 3 2 1

Contents

Foreword

There is something beautiful about Black boys. As children, they play in innocence, whisper in imagination, and sing in colors of joy. Yet historical and contemporary accounts of Black boys in schools too often mask the sublime with pejorative narratives of deficit and danger. We know so little of these boys' early academic dispositions because stereotypes and misinformation hide their realities. Educators, researchers, and policy leaders are implicated in dimming the sparkle of Black boys' potential and possibility, as well as in shaping how the public understands them. For instance, images and discourses that construct Black boys as problems distort their actual in- and out-of-school lives. While these problem-making mechanisms are generally external to Black boys, their consequences become the burdens these boys face in school and society. However, early childhood education (PK–3rd grade) as a field of practice, research, and policy does not have to be limited by frameworks and expectations that diminish the radiance of these children. *The Brilliance of Black Boys: Cultivating School Success in the Early Grades* claims new ground to advance knowledge and practice that can change the narrative about Black boys and their early schooling. With this purpose in mind, Brian L. Wright and Shelly L. Counsell offer a book that challenges and outlines a path of transformation for how schools and the broader society think about, engage with, and foster success for Black boys.

The growing expansion of social science research focusing on Black boys brings needed attention to this population. New scholarship that moves away from stereotypical problem-based themes and toward broader conceptions and considerations of Black boys is duly necessary. *The Brilliance of Black Boys* expands our knowing of Black boys and in turn holds schools and educators accountable for responding to these new understandings. For instance, the increasing use of narratives questioning stale assumptions of academic engagement and growth enliven scholarship that has for too long succumbed to traditional notions about school readiness and social competencies of these young learners. Drawing on empirical evidence and best practices, *The Brilliance of Black Boys* should make many uncomfortable and motivate others to do better.

Another important contribution of *The Brilliance of Black Boys* is the advancement of anti-deficit thinking about Black boys and asset-based approaches to research and practice. The authors' achievement framework helps in changing the narrative and challenging research on Black boys, especially in discussions about school readiness. To be honest, I have been waiting for this book. My anticipation was not based on the complete absence of approaches that emphasize strengths and assets in educations; a number of scholars engage in this kind of work across the education pipeline with a variety of student groups. However, my excitement about this book comes from its audacity to assert a perspective about the early education of Black boys that centers their cultural authenticity inclusive of identity, agency, and lived experiences. This is an ambitious undertaking, but early childhood education desperately needs it to enact its broader goals of igniting intellectual curiosity, cultivating social competencies, and supporting the sociocultural development of *all* children.

The Brilliance of Black Boys fills both important scholarly and practice gaps in discerning boys' experience in early childhood education at the intersection of race and gender. Not limited to challenging the conventional constructions and stereotypes of Black boys, the book additionally serves as a barometer and guide for how schools reconsider whom these students are, with attention to their prior knowledge and experience. For sure, the role of early childhood education is so consequential in the development of Black boys and in how they begin to see themselves and their contributions in the world. While difficult to imagine, the potential social casualties of doing this improperly could haunt us for generations. Thus, the risk is too great for continuing to denying Black boys access to appropriate and sustaining early learning opportunities.

Explaining how to build a culture of success for Black boys is a central objective of *The Brilliance of Black Boys*. By introducing a conceptual frame to improve the success of Black boys, Wright and Counsell argue for classrooms and curricula integration of cultural markers, identity exploration and the lived experiences of Black boys. Notably, the authors posit a cultural responsiveness and competence in teaching Black boys—one that considers unique racial-gender awareness and promotes congruent learning strategies, such as using more mirror books rather than window books and revisiting questions about who counts as a "good student." This unapologetic call for centering the social, cultural, and language practices of Black boys is a core contribution of this book, but its implications go beyond the role of teachers, curricula, and school culture. The effect of recognizing and honoring the authenticity of Black boys holds the possibility of reorienting early childhood education to become more inclusive and meaningful. Placing Black boys at the center of understanding who they are, and what and how they learn in early education, affords opportunities for genuine discovery and development.

Creating these nurturing early education environments of self-discovery and social awareness, where Black boys can imagine, learn, love, and grow is critical, given the constraints that society and educational institutions will impose. Based on this timely text, I am encouraged that early education can be intentional in its objective to acknowledge and affirm the lives of Black boys. I am also convinced that early childhood educators and the culture of schools can serve Black boys effectively. As a result, we can begin to actualize early schooling as a site for the effective development of social identities and competencies of Black boys—aligned with who they are and their possible selves.

At this historical moment when political rhetoric of ridicule captures the daily attention of the American public, the affirming study and practice of early childhood education with attention to race and gender is even more important. This work increases my faith in the possibility of ensuring Black boys lives of joy and wonder. We can guarantee them the simple beauty of being children rather than objectified "little men." Illuminating the light of Black boys is all of our responsibility, and *The Brilliance of Black Boys* gets us closer to a village that sees, respects, educates, and cares for them.

—James Earl Davis

Acknowledgments

To write a book about Black boys that challenges prevailing deficit views that exist in schools and society in hopes of shifting the narrative from "at risk" to "at promise" is to recognize and invest in the brilliance that we know resides in Black boys. We first acknowledge Sarah Biondello, senior acquisition editor at Teachers College Press, who believed in this project right from the start. Thanks to John Bylander, our production editor, whose conscientious approach helped to maintain the book's indispensable message that Black boys deserve the same protection, nurturing, and support as other children.

The social–emotional well-being of Black boys must be of the utmost priority in order to see them, hear them, and know them, and to provide them with schooling that is humane, culturally responsive, and anti-deficit. With this charge and expectation in mind, a very special thanks goes to James Earl Davis, professor and Bernard C. Watson Endowed Chair in Urban Education at Temple University, who, when invited to write the foreword, enthusiastically agreed.

To our colleagues in the Department of Instruction and Curriculum Leadership (ICL) at the University of Memphis, we thank you for your words of encouragement, your support, and the space and time to write and complete this book. To Jasmine Morton, thank you for your meticulous organization and preparation of the master reference list.

Thanks goes to DeAnna McClendon (Shelby County Schools), Karen Harrell (Porter-Leath), and LaQuita Cole and Crystal Blackmon (Early Childhood Academy) for working with their staff to obtain permission from families of the children featured on the cover of this book (photograph courtesy of Porter-Leath). A note of thanks to Terrance Riley (a lead teacher at Early Childhood Academy) for permission to photograph him conducting a class meeting with his students featured in Chapter 5. Thanks to the Barbara K. Lipman Early Childhood School and Research Institute at the University of Memphis for permission to include photographs of their students and student work featured in Chapter 5. Finally, we would like to thank the Regents' Center for Early Development Education at the University of Northern Iowa for permission to use photographs of children engaged in Ramps and Pathways also featured in Chapter 5.

A very special thanks goes to Donna Y. Ford, professor and Cornelius Vanderbilt Endowed Chair at Vanderbilt University, for her critical and contemplative questions, firm prodding, and brilliant sense of structure, all of which have made this book more compelling.

I, Brian, acknowledge with gratitude a community of diverse scholars, colleagues, and friends who have nurtured my intellectual growth and scholarly development. They include, but are not limited to: Shirley S. Winstead, Mona W. Thornton, Matilda Martin, Barbara Graham, Elaine P. Witty, Constantine Georgiou (deceased), Calvin "Chip" Gidney, III (chair of my dissertation committee), Jayanthi Mistry (co-chair of my dissertation committee), Ellen E. Pinderhughes, Richard M. Lerner, Betty Allen, Justina Clayton, Janie V. Ward (dissertation committee member), Theresa Perry (dissertation committee member), Denise Patmon, Vivian L. Gadsden, Beth Warren, Ann Rosebery, Sabina Vaught, Karen Belcher-Harris, Monique F. Brinson, and Sneha Veeragoudar Harrell.

I also acknowledge the love, continuous support, and encouragement of my family. To my parents, Elton M. Skeeter Wright and William "Harold" Wright, thank you. To my siblings, Barry H. Wright, Terrie A. Wright, and Adrian L. Wright, I send my continued love. To my nieces Shaila M. Wood, Taahirah Wright, and Arie R. Wright: You represent three brilliant Black girls. And to my nephew, Muhammad Wright, a brilliant Black boy: May you always claim and assert your brilliance out in the world. This book is dedicated to the memory of my grandmother Mrs. Blanche V. Wright (1912–2003), who, through her wisdom, taught me to look, linger, and learn.

I, Shelly, acknowledge the loving care, genuine interest, compassion, encouragement, and relentless support of my partner, Ron Counsell; our daughters, Kimberly Wheelock and Kristen Counsell; my mother, Beverly Weigle; and my mother-in-law, Elizabeth Counsell. I am forever indebted to Robert Boody, my dissertation co-chair, and the late Rheta DeVries, a dissertation committee member; together, they actively nurtured and challenged my growth and development as a constructivist and critical scholar, researcher, and educator. Last, but arguably most important, I draw my courage, inspiration, and conviction for completing this project from the Black boys I have had the pleasure to teach and their families. I am a far better teacher, advocate, and human being because of them.

Finally, we dedicate this book to the exceptional intelligence, ability, prowess, skill, aptitude, flair, finesse, panache, greatness, and radiance that is *The Brilliance of Black Boys*.

Introduction

Why is there a need for a book about Black boys in the early grades (pre-kindergarten through 3rd grade)? We write about Black boys because we seek to challenge and transform the way schools and society think, talk, research, and write about this population. Moreover, we write about Black boys using counter-narratives from an anti-deficit perspective in order to push back against the prevalence of deficit-oriented discourse that exists about these students. We also write about Black boys because the inequalities that they experience in educational environments manifest in early childhood and, if unaddressed, are compounded during their later schooling and life (Wright, 2016).

It is well documented that high-quality school experiences play a critically important role in increasing the life chances of African American boys. However, creating more culturally responsive and responsible educational experiences (and outcomes) for Black children in general, and boys in particular, remains a challenge for many school officials. African American boys know all too well what it feels like to be viewed as a "problem" in school. Sadly, it is no secret among African American men and boys that people are often afraid of them and believe that they are not doing well in school or society. In fact, there is a plethora of empirical evidence highlighting the challenges African American boys encounter in education and the consequences associated with the presumption that this population is in complete peril. This discourse about the social and academic lives of Black boys as incapable of catching up to the culture of schools and not the other way around (e.g., excelling in certain contexts) is a stubborn narrative. This deficit-laden discourse is amply documented in the extant literature on the academic achievement gap, which is replete with dismal statistics of the persistent academic underachievement of African American boys, pre-K–12. On the one hand, it is important to acknowledge the full extent of the challenges that African American boys face as they seek to be educated in U.S. schools. On the other hand, too much emphasis on problems versus promise and potential can lead to the misconception that all or most Black boys are failing in school, which suppresses solutions, especially those that accentuate and validate the strengths, promise, and potential of African American boys, beginning in early childhood.

BLACK BOYHOOD INTERRUPTED AND
DISRUPTED IN EARLY CHILDHOOD

As we discuss in greater detail throughout this book, negative stereotypical perceptions of Black boys begin as early as preschool and kindergarten, where their behaviors often are "adultified" and "criminalized" during the early and later stages of childhood (Wright, Ford, & Grantham, 2018). Black boys barely out of diapers are being viewed and treated as if they are much older. "Their transgressions are made to take on a sinister, intentional, fully conscious tone that is stripped of any element of childish naïveté" (Ferguson, 2000, p. 83). These constructions often lead to racialized and gendered classroom experiences that are hostile and have short-term and long-term harmful effects on Black boys. This is evidenced by the disproportionately high rates of suspension and expulsion for Black boys compared with White children, as discussed in Chapter 1. This alone is cause for serious pause with regard to the role that race and gender play in the lives of this population, regardless of students' ages. It is little wonder that these racial disparities in discipline and suspensions have a devastating impact on how Black boys are portrayed and treated in society and in the scholarly literature as "bad boys" and "troublemakers."

These and other reasons, delineated and interrogated in this book, are why we choose to focus on Black boys in the early grades from an anti-deficit perspective (promise, potential, and possibilities) rather than continuing more of the same when it comes to the discourse and dialogue with, on, and about this young population. By our exploration of these topics, we aim to help schools first and foremost and, by extension, society better understand Black boys so that they will be seen as boys and not men, and will be allowed simply to be children with promise, potential, and possibilities. But, first, we introduce the conceptual framework of success for Black boys that guides this work.

CONCEPTUAL FRAMEWORK OF SUCCESS FOR BLACK BOYS

For many African American boys, there exists a mismatch between content taught in the classroom and their lived experiences outside of school. This mismatch between children's home cultures and the cultures of schools wreaks havoc with student achievement. Given that culture shapes how children understand life and their connection to the world as well as "how" and "what" they learn, creating equitable (fair and impartial) early childhood classrooms that recognize, nurture, and integrate the home cultures of African American boys is critical (Nasir, Rosebery, Warren, & Lee, 2006). The important role for the early childhood teacher, then, is to structure learning opportunities for African American boys that will complement their cultural worlds of home. We believe that if the cultural and personal identities of African American boys are recognized, nurtured, and fully integrated into the classroom, their lived experiences and funds of knowledge can be treated equally in school. We use the phrase "funds of knowledge" to mean the various social, cultural, and linguistic practices that are essential to the lives of African American boys.

Guided by these assertions, our claims are grounded in and informed by the following theoretical/conceptual frameworks: (1) sociocultural theory (Lee, Spencer, & Harpalani, 2003; Rogoff, 2003); (2) anti-deficit achievement framework (Harper, 2010); and (3) culturally responsive teaching (Gay, 2010; Hammond, 2015). Taken together, these three theoretical/conceptual frameworks are used specifically to help conceptualize, describe, and explain how the complex intersection of social, cultural, and linguistic practices can either advance or impede the learning, growth, and development of African American boys inside and outside of school settings.

Sociocultural theory is used to explain how learning results directly from social interactions among the individual, society, and culture. Using this approach, we argue that African American boys can succeed in school if teachers create more equitable and culturally responsive classrooms (as defined in Chapter 1) to give them the same advantage that White, middle-class children always seem to have. In other words, we advocate for equitable and culturally responsive early childhood classrooms that place the knowledge and experiences of African American boys at the center of teaching and learning.

To further explain our point of view, we draw upon and ground our claims in an anti-deficit achievement framework (ADAF). This approach seeks to disrupt the prevalence of the deficit-oriented narrative around African American boys' lives in and outside of school. Harper (2012) explains that the ADAF "inverts questions that are commonly asked about educational disadvantage, underrepresentation, insufficient preparation, academic underperformance, disengagement, and Black male student attrition" (p. 5). For instance, instead of asking deficit-oriented questions like, Why are Black boys not succeeding academically and socially in school?, an ADAF question would ask, How do Black boys from low-resourced schools manage to succeed in school? and/or, What can teachers do to create a match between the home cultures of African American boys and the cultures of school in order to maximize their assets and strengths (Harper & Associates, 2014)? In essence, we use ADAF to provide teachers with a mindset for asking anti-deficit questions instead of relying on questions that amplify deficits, underachievement, and stereotypes. By inverting deficit-laden questions, teachers are put in the position to challenge prevailing and unexamined attitudes, beliefs, and practices that have largely focused on the perceived deficits of the experiences of African American boys instead of their assets and strengths.

Finally, our claims are grounded in the importance of culturally responsive teaching, which entails "using the cultural knowledge, prior experiences, frames of references, and performance styles of ethnically diverse students to make learning encounters more relevant to and effective for them" (Gay, 2010, p. 31). As explained by Hammond (2015):

> Being responsive to diverse students' needs asks teachers to be mindful and present. That requires reflection. Engaging in reflection helps culturally responsive teachers recognize the beliefs, behaviors, and practices that get in the way of their ability to respond constructively and positively to students. (p. 53)

The overarching premise of CRT, then, hinges on the idea that culture as both situated and situational is a critical component to achieving equitable learning experiences for children in general—and African American boys in particular. The intellectual merit and impact of culturally responsive teaching are fully actualized when teachers recognize that they "are not a neutral party in the [teaching and learning] process" (Hammond, 2015, p. 53). In other words, teachers are always implicated in the school success of their students.

The following sections provide an overview of each chapter's focus. We begin, however, with a note about terminology and a perspective to shift the mindset of how Black boys typically are framed.

A NOTE ABOUT TERMINOLOGY AND PERSPECTIVE

We use the terms *Black boy(s)* and *African American boy(s)* interchangeably. We choose not to use "Black males" or "African American males," to emphasize that we are writing about children, from prekindergarten to 3rd grade (early childhood). We want to remind readers that the Black boys we are talking about are *not* men. They are still *very* young and need, like all other children pre-K–12, guidance, support, encouragement, and love. We reject the use of the phrases "Black males" and "African American males," which are used regularly in the media and in social science research in ways that subconsciously and consciously dehumanize, criminalize, and "adultify" members of this population as a monolithic group, making them into a clinical statistical category. Framing members of this population in this way, we argue, contributes to the police treating them like men (e.g., 12-year-old Tamir Rice); the judicial system treating them like men; and teachers as early as preschool fearing them like they would fear adult men, or expecting them to have skills of code-switching (e.g., assimilation into mainstream ways of knowing and being) and racial border crossing (e.g., expertise about other people's cultures) that most adults do not have (Moore, Michael, & Penick-Parks, 2018, p. 7).

To corroborate our claim, a 2014 study (discussed in detail in Chapter 4) conducted by Goff, Jackson, Di Leone, Culotta, and DiTomasso, titled "The Essence of Innocence: Consequences of Dehumanizing Black Children," published by the American Psychological Association, found that Black boys as young as 10 years old may not be viewed in the same light of childhood innocence as their White peers. Instead, these boys are more likely to be mistaken as older, be perceived as guilty, and face police violence if accused of a crime. With such issues in mind, we aim to challenge this universal framing by acknowledging that Black boys are *not* men and that being Black and male *are not* risk factors nor are the differences that may be exhibited by this group evidence of deficiency. To counter this pervasive view, we intentionally take a strengths-based look at the state of Black boys in early childhood. We aim to celebrate, honor, and cherish Black boys. They are not inherently at risk; rather, they are placed at risk through no fault of their own. We will show through vignettes, stories, and other data that the innocence of Black boys lies in their natural curiosity, excitement, and genius, which must be recognized, understood, encouraged, supported, and protected.

"Ambivalent about reporting yet again on these widespread academic underachievement patterns" (Nasir, 2012, p. 2), the authors of this book avoid deficit models in favor of a focus that recognizes, understands, and cultivates the diversity of social skills of African American boys in the early grades. Reframing the knowledge, skills, and cultural resources displayed in early childhood classrooms by African American boys as examples of their competent adaptive responses and practices can and does contribute to a healthy self-identity that has the potential to facilitate personal agency toward the school success of this population.

When African American boys are recognized as having assets versus deficits, the potential for changes in perspectives, attitudes, and beliefs by those who work with this population—early childhood teachers, the majority of whom are White and female—is increased. One of our main goals is to challenge deficit perspectives by accentuating cognitive, academic, psychological, physical, and social skills/competencies used by young African American boys to negotiate and navigate between their multiple cultural worlds of home, community, and school.

Again, we reject the all too familiar deficit view of African American boys' early development (pre-K–3rd grade) in favor of a strengths-based view, using sensitive and culturally responsive practices, that celebrates the socioemotional development and learning of Black boys. Finally, we assert that a strengths-based (anti-deficit) view can provide insight into how African American boys construct and co-construct personal meaning for their social and academic lives. Guided by these assertions, we provide vignettes of African American boys (pre-K–3rd grade) at the start of each chapter to illustrate what is lost when Black boys are not allowed or even encouraged to participate freely in boyhood (normatively and ethnically, specifically) but instead must attend to adult and peer interactions and attitudes that view them as "bad boys" and "troublemakers."

In order to move beyond deficit-oriented perspectives about African American boys that begin in early childhood, the authors invite early childhood professionals to ponder these two questions:

1. What would it mean for African American boys to thrive in early childhood classrooms?
2. What would it look like for African American boys to thrive in early childhood classrooms?

REFRAMING THE NARRATIVE ABOUT BLACK BOYS IN EARLY CHILDHOOD

There is a growing body of seminal and contemporary research that documents the social competencies that African American boys bring to their educational experiences in the older grades. Absent, however, are studies that focus on the social competencies and cultural resources of African American boys in early childhood education (pre-K–3rd grade). For this reason, this book highlights examples (anecdotal and empirical) that focus on African American boys in pre-K–3rd grade. The subsequent chapters generally explore these questions:

1. What social competencies do African American boys use to negotiate and navigate the schooling context?
2. What type of supports at home and school facilitate their ability to negotiate and navigate school?

OVERVIEW

We begin Chapter 1 with a vignette titled *"What Are Little Boys Made of?"* to explore the experiences of Black boys in and outside of school. We then start a discussion that acknowledges and challenges what is already known and repeatedly reproduced about the situation and circumstances of Black boys. Statistics and other data are used to contextualize the experiences of Black boys in and outside of school. These data make explicit how Black boys are positioned as a group, differently from other boys of color and White boys. In this chapter, we establish the importance of understanding the racialized, gendered, and sociocultural relationship between Black boys, schools, and society. This book aims to change the narrative for Black boys in early childhood in a concerted effort to improve not only their schooling experiences, but their life outcomes as well. We conclude the chapter with a focus on strengths and assets versus deficits, making the case for why this fundamental shift is critical to answering not only the question, "What are Black boys made of?" but also, "How do we change the narrative for Black boys early in their schooling, pre-K–3rd grade?"

Chapter 2 begins with a vignette titled *"Karl Is Ready. Are You?"* We examine more closely the idea of being ready for school, through a critical discussion on school readiness. The remainder of the chapter focuses on the schooling experience of Black boys in general, and in early childhood in particular. We highlight the ways that schools approach the teaching of African American boys as a daunting and insurmountable challenge. Consequently, in many schools attended by Black boys, beginning in early childhood, the maintenance of order and discipline is the focus rather than the students' learning, positive self-identity, and academic achievement. As a result, by the time Black boys reach 3rd or 4th grade, their teachers and other school personnel no longer treat them like children, but rather like men. This begins the perpetuation of stereotypes about Black boys as dangerous, lazy, dishonest, violent, athletic, and unintelligent (T. C. Howard, 2014; Ladson-Billings, 2011; Wright, 2009). Building on the previous chapter, we offer a counter-narrative to the pervasive dominant narratives of "troublemaker," "bad boy," and the view that Black boys are "unready" for school; our approach emphasizes strengths and assets rather than problems and deficits.

We begin Chapter 3 with a vignette titled *"This Little Light of Mine"* to further explain what happens when schools acknowledge and use only a limited range of the kinds of talk, thinking, and interactional styles that Black boys use in their everyday lives. This narrowness serves to marginalize much of what children in general, and Black boys in particular, learn in their homes and communities as irrelevant to school. In contrast to this limited (and limiting) view that dominates the Black boys' narrative, we accentuate ways to create "cultures of success" by capitalizing on, and actively engaging, the strengths and assets of diverse talk, thinking (sense-making practices), and interactional styles within culturally responsive and culturally respectful early childhood classroom settings.

When teachers actively listen to, openly acknowledge, and value children's prior knowledge, learning interests, agendas, and ideas, they become "fellow travelers" who co-construct meanings with children through a shared learning journey of growth and empowerment (Counsell & Boody, 2013; Smith, 2012; Wright, Counsell, & Tate, 2015, 2016). As fellow travelers in the creation of a democratic learning community, teachers and children work together to define how they want to think, speak, act, learn, and grow together. Democratic classrooms, as described by Kohn (2006), promote cultures of success with the view that *all* students are community members (equity) with the opportunity to (1) have a voice in what happens; (2) help shape the course of study; (3) help decide when, where, why, how, and with whom learning takes place; and (4) help decide how progress will be assessed. The learning environment is then designed so young children can explore what interests them and direct their own activity and decision making (empowerment and agency) by selecting materials and participating in activities in a variety of social arrangements (independent, pairs, small group, and whole group).

This chapter demonstrates the strengths, benefits, and advantages of creating cultures of success that, in turn, maximize learner (as well as life opportunity) outcomes. Cultures of success (in and outside of school settings) rely heavily on the strength and ability of culturally competent and responsive mentors who are well prepared to guide, facilitate, and support the learning and development of young Black boys in their everyday lives. In summary, this chapter serves to further question the overrepresentation of Black boys in special education and the school-to-prison pipeline (life outcome) that often are directly attributed to school "cultures of deficit."

Chapter 4 begins with a vignette titled *"Why Ryheim Does Not Like to Read"* that introduces, explains, and discusses the concepts of healthy "self-identity" and "agency." The self-identity construct answers the question, "Who am I?" as it relates to children in general, and Black boys in particular. Similarly, agency as a construct answers the questions, "What actions can I take?" and "Will my actions make a difference?" Agency is explored as it relates to children's ability in general to act upon their cultural worlds of home and school. This examination includes the contradictions that Black boys encounter when they are allowed and encouraged to construct and co-construct their environment at home and in their community in contrast to the reality they face in formal school settings. At school, Black boys must negotiate different courses of action in their use of agency (as defined by conventionally accepted and unaccepted mores of behavior) that can lead to either "healthy" or "unhealthy" (deficit) self-identities. Black boys' identities are further reinscribed and reinforced by teachers, who clearly play a key role in children's socialization, learning, and development. This chapter will utilize authentic multicultural children's literature as one way to foster healthy self-identity and agency in Black boys. Ultimately the aim of this chapter is to see Black boys as competent learners, with an emphasis on their promise, potential, and possibilities that cannot be ignored and must not be stifled.

Opening the conversation with a vignette titled *"They (My White Teachers) . . . ,"* Chapter 5 explores the missed or lost opportunities for Black boys when schools and society fail to see and comprehend Black boys' strengths, assets, promise, potential, and possibilities. To address this urgent and glaring dilemma, the chapter discusses effective classroom strategies used to promote self-identity and agency by celebrating Black boys' strengths, assets, and promise, ultimately leading to school (and life) success. Effective democratic learning communities rely heavily on community members' development of self-identity and their ability to exercise agency. Culturally responsive practices and strategies like mirror books (rather than the dominant window books) and a variety of empowerment clubs (just to name a few) support and promote Black boys' positive self-identity development within cultures of success.

In essence, this chapter aims to help teachers and all those who care about the education of Black boys to acknowledge that "different is not deficient" (Emdin, 2012) and to "stop pretending that all students are alike; teaching to their differences [as strengths and assets] will improve their chances for academic success" (p. 13). Vignettes, stories, statistics, and other data are used throughout this book to help guide, inform, and reinforce the critical need for a counter-narrative about Black boys' strengths and assets. Creating a "new" narrative of empowerment and success for Black boys calls into question previous notions, attitudes, and assumptions about the unexamined norms of what counts as a "good student." This new narrative, in turn, further expands upon and transforms a newly revised "good student" narrative as a crucial and central tenet within democratic cultures of success.

The Appendix offers a list of general and specific resources for building cultural competence in early childhood teachers so they can work effectively with Black boys in early education and care settings (pre-K–3rd grade). The various resources included in the Appendix are as follows: (1) academic/professional journals, (2) authentic multicultural children's books with Black boys as protagonists, (3) early childhood/child development websites for teachers, (4) professional associations/organizations and related conferences and symposia, (5) education centers and institutes, (6) research reports on Black males, (7) Black male teacher initiatives, and (8) an example of a current Black male initiative. Our hope is that teacher educators, teachers, and all those who care about the education of Black boys will find these resources useful in supporting their schooling, learning, and social–emotional development.

CHAPTER 1

Black Boys' Experiences
in School and out of School

> What are little boys made of?
> Snips and snails, and puppy dogs' tails
> That's what little boys are made of.
>
> —The Real Mother Goose (1916)

Is there a Black boy in your world to whom the 19th-century nursery rhyme can be applied regarding *"what little boys are made of"*? This rhyme attempted to capture an idyllic view of childhood in general, and boyhood in particular, but had little to do with Black boys then or now in the 21st century. The latter claim is based partially on the persistent adultification of Black children. *Adultification* is defined as "a social or cultural stereotype that is based on how adults perceive children in the absence of knowledge of children's behavior and verbalization . . . which is based in part on race [and gender]" (Epstein, Blake, & González, 2017, p. 4). To contextualize this definition for the purposes of this book, we assert that, even when adults have knowledge of child development (e.g., children's behavior and interactional styles), the adultification of Black children persists. For Black boys, adultification is based in large part on the culpability that has historically been ascribed to individuals of their race and gender by schools and society.

Evidence of the adultification and criminalization of Black boys and girls is corroborated in studies conducted by Goff et al. (2014) and Epstein et al. (2017). In the study by Goff and colleagues titled "The Essence of Innocence: Consequences of Dehumanizing Black Children" published in the *Journal of Personality and Social Psychology*, it was found that participants overestimated the age of Black boys by an average of 4.5 years and considered them more culpable than Whites or Latinos, particularly when the boys were matched with serious crimes. That analysis also revealed that participants who implicitly associated Blacks with apes thought the Black children were older and less innocent than their White peers. In fact, the implicit dehumanization of Blacks was a significant predictor of racial disparities in the use of force against children (Goff et al., 2014).

In the study by Epstein and colleagues titled "Girlhood Interrupted: The Erasure of Black Girls' Childhood" published by the Georgetown Law Center on Poverty and Inequality, it was found that Black girls also are viewed as less innocent and more adult-like than their White peers. In fact, a snapshot of the data revealed that, compared with White peers, Black girls as early as 5 years of age were perceived as needing less nurturing, protection, support, and comfort; being more independent; and knowing more about adult topics and sex (Epstein et al., 2017).

Both studies are profound and troubling, with far-reaching implications that, without a doubt, contribute to disparities in educational and social settings. As early childhood professionals, we are saddened by Black boys being "convicted in the womb" (Upchurch, 1997) as early in life as upon entering school.

BLACK BOYS IN SCHOOL AND OUT OF SCHOOL

Inside schools, Black boys are subject to harsher discipline, resulting in their overrepresentation at early ages and grade levels in suspension and expulsion, and high incidence in areas of special education. These academic disparities, discussed below in greater detail, are inextricably linked to negative life outcomes (social, environmental, academic). These outcomes include economic hardships due to high rates of unemployment and discrimination in various sectors of the job market, adverse health conditions, drug and alcohol abuse, negative media perceptions, racial hate-crime violence, and victimization as a result of police violence (Anderson, 2008; Caldwell, Kohn-Wood, Schmeelk-Cone, Chavous, & Zimmerman, 2004; Davis, 2005; Ferguson, 2000; Graves, 2008; Harper, Terry, & Twiggs, 2009; T. C. Howard, 2008, 2014; Irvine, 1990; Morial, 2007; Noguera, 2003; Thompson, 2002; Wright, 2011a, 2017).

These critical academic, social, and environmental issues are used time and again to blame and demonize Black boys and their families for their "failures" and, likewise, to justify and perpetuate, to some extent, the adultification, criminalization, and mis-education of this population because its members are considered "unteachable" and therefore needing to be controlled (i.e., disciplined) at all costs, especially under zero-tolerance policies. These deficit views and the practice of "blaming the victim," we argue, conveniently subvert the focus on race(ism) and discrimination. The tendency to absolve individuals and institutions of any and all responsibility regarding the academic and environmental disparities facing Black boys ignores, negates, and trivializes the multitude of economic and societal inequities that produce these systemic problems (see Milner, 2010, 2015). The correlation between the dehumanization of both Black boys and their experiences in and outside of school becomes even more significant when consideration is given to the fact that, routinely and without reservation, the presumption of childhood innocence and protection is afforded White children but categorically denied to Black boys of all ages and backgrounds (e.g., high income, low income, gifted and talented, special education, urban, rural, suburban).

Against this lethal backdrop of troubling circumstances, we must revise the nursery rhyme to ask: *"What are little Black boys made of?"* "Gloom and doom" statistics as the primary narrative told to and about Black boys inevitably leads to another question: What happens when these troubling circumstances limit the promise, gifts and talents, potential, and possibilities of Black boys? This is the case when Black boys (e.g., Tamir Rice, a 12-year-old African American boy) are denied "leniency when determining the consequences of their behavior" (Epstein et al., 2017, p. 2) "at the hands of police officers, security guards and self-appointed vigilantes" (O'Bryant, 2014, p. 1).

These questions, assertions, and harsh realities can affect Black boys at any point in their development, including, unfortunately, as early as preschool, when they are barely out of diapers. How do we support the school readiness and success of Black boys in light of these harsh realities? How do we ensure that Black boys are allowed to be children in a society that will see them as innocent or deserving of protection, when the reality is that their society finds them guilty before even considering them innocent?

In subsequent sections, using national data (U.S. Department of Education Office for Civil Rights, 2014), we frame issues such as disproportionate suspension and expulsion rates as reflective of racialized and gendered practices that have contributed to a gross inequity, and we explain what we mean by culturally responsive and responsible early childhood education for Black boys. We home in on what it means to teach other people's children (Delpit, 1995, 2006) as if they were our own and/or as we would like our children to be treated in schools. We conclude with recommendations for achieving equitable early childhood experiences for Black boys.

By equitable early childhood experiences, we mean the use of culturally responsive and responsible educational practices and democratic classroom environments that validate, empower, and situate the cultural and self-identities of African American boys to promote their personal and cultural agency. These practices are informed and shaped by various research-based best practices (going beyond developmentally appropriate practices) to support the school readiness and success of young African American boys. To achieve these aims, it is important that educators and the larger society understand that too much focus on "gloom and doom" statistics ignores the humanity of Black boys in terms of what they want and need: to be nurtured, protected, and supported as children, fellow human beings, and those under our care as trained education professionals.

CONSEQUENCES OF PERCEPTIONS OF CULPABILITY OF BLACK BOYS

In a hard-hitting, cut-to-the-chase, autobiographical book, Upchurch (1997) lamented and bemoaned that far too many Black boys are convicted in the womb. Like Upchurch and others, we condemn zero-tolerance policies and the predictable school-to-prison pipeline (Alexander, 2010; Barbarin, 2013; T. C. Howard, 2014; Losen & Gillespie, 2012; Wright, 2016). Sadly, Black families have come to expect that when they send their son off to school (including preschool), he may repeatedly experience cultural assaults on his identity, potential, and character, resulting in frustration and uncomfortable or alienating schooling experiences that extend out into the world. Moreover, their Black son may encounter expectations at the hands of well-meaning teachers that are at odds with his culturally based development; this may leave him bewildered and wondering, "What am I made of?" Although a simple question, the answers for Black boys vary and are complicated along lines of race, class, gender, ability, and disability; this raises another critical question: "Who is the young Black male child in the 21st century?"

EDUCATION DENIED: STATISTICS ON SUSPENSIONS AND EXPULSION

African American preschool children are 3.6 times as likely to receive one or more out-of-school suspensions as White preschool children. In fact, while Black boys represent only 19% of the male preschool enrollment, they represent 45% of the male preschool children receiving one or more out-of-school suspensions. By comparison, White children represent 41% of preschool enrollment, but only 28% of preschool children receiving one or more out-of-school suspensions (U.S. Department of Education Office for Civil Rights, 2016). Beginning in preschool—a time when children are actively constructing meaning about their cultural worlds, and that is marked by social, imaginative, and active play—African American boys encounter teachers who tend to stigmatize them, giving them negative labels, such as "bad boy" or "troublemaker." Such labels often are passed along from teacher to teacher throughout the schooling process (Wright, Counsell, & Tate, 2015; Wright & Ford, 2016b).

These labels also lead to isolation and exclusion from classroom activities and begin the practices of adultification, underrepresentation in gifted education, and overrepresentation in special education (i.e., both misidentification and misplacement in high-incidence categories of emotional and behavior disorders, intellectual disability, learning disability, and developmental delay) that characterize the schooling experiences of far too many pre-K–12 African American boys (Wright & Ford, 2016a, 2017a).

Against this backdrop of racial disproportionalities also exists the egregious school-to-prison pipeline. For example, research has shown that Black boys, in particular, often are perceived as less innocent and more adultlike than their White male peers. As a result, they are more likely to be assigned greater culpability for their actions (in or outside of school), which increases their risk of contact with the juvenile justice system. The Schott Foundation revealed how Black students are far more likely to be suspended or expelled than their White peers—actually more likely than all other students, regardless of gender, race, and income. These disparities begin the process of pushing students out of school at very young ages (pre-K–3) and hindering their opportunities to access high-quality early education (prekindergarten) and their overall educational experiences once they enter the pre-K–12 system. Focusing on the importance of early education programs, a report from the Center for American Progress (Adamu & Hogan, 2015) makes it clear that schools implementing these programs need to be aware of the dangers of harsh and unjust disciplinary practices that contribute significantly to the school-to-prison pipeline. School officials must be mindful and vigilant about racial and gender inequities.

RACE AND GENDER IN THE CLASSROOM

As previously discussed, the unique challenges and complex ways in which structural and systemic racism in society and schools shapes the experiences and well-being of Black boys, including implicit bias and explicit forms of racism, must be understood and aggressively addressed to disrupt the adultification and criminalization of behaviors of Black boys.

Race and gender often circumscribe the educational experiences and opportunities of African American students, especially "Black males [who] are too often disadvantaged by this perplexing and misunderstood intersection of race and gender" (J. E. Davis, 2005, p. 131). For this reason, a deeper understanding of the relationship between these social position factors is required. Ritualized expressions of masculinity among Black boys can intersect or interact negatively with race in the context of school. That is, racialized manifestations of Black masculinity often are viewed as "oppositional" to the culture of school. Examples of this include "such things as dress (for example, beltless pants hanging below the waist), manner of talk (signifying, rapping), and behavior (high fives, special handshakes, forms of greeting)" (Tatum, 2005, p. 29).

School personnel who are unaware that these expressions of Black masculinity (e.g., cool pose, swagger) are the norm within their culture often engage Black boys with deficit thinking—suspicion, fear, and negativity. This mindset and associated treatment can contribute to Black boys adopting less than favorable attitudes regarding schools and society and their place in both (Wright, 2009). On this very point, Tatum (2005) wrote: "Black males respond to schooling based on both their perception of the treatment they receive in school and their perceptions of what schooling will do for them in the future" (p. 73). Therefore, when educators respond negatively to styles of personal and cultural presentation of Black boys (e.g., questioning, talking, walking, dress, hair) by imposing strict rules and prohibitions, they are communicating a message of rejection, which can contribute to students' psychological discomfort and low academic achievement (T. C. Howard, 2014).

Understanding the educational status and trajectory of Black boys of all ages has a long history, with a few key studies and reports such as *The Counter Narrative* by Tyrone C. Howard and Associates (2017), *Succeeding in the City* by Shaun Harper and Associates (2014), and *Breaking Barriers* by Ivory Toldson (2008). These studies (see Appendix for a complete list of resources) document positive experiences and outcomes. Journals such as *Journal of African American Males in Education* and *Spectrum: A Journal on Black Men*, organizations such as My Brother's Keeper and the Schott Foundation, and special interest forums such as Educating Black Boys and Adolescent Males have been created to advocate for this one group of students.

Terms such as *endangered* and *at risk* have become a proxy for "Black boys." Figure 1.1 presents a quick snapshot of key issues that dominate the discourse, dialogue, and writings about Black boys. Despite the efforts by Howard, Harper, Toldson, and others, we are still left to question whether it is possible for educators and society to see Black children—in this case, boys—any other way than as problems. Answering this question requires an examination of teachers' attitudes of and expectations for Black boys.

Figure 1.1. Status of Black Boys in Education: Discipline, Special Education, Gifted Education

DISCIPLINE and ZERO TOLERANCE Overrepresentation	• Office referrals • Suspensions • Expulsions
SPECIAL EDUCATION (High-Incidence Categories) Overrepresentation	• Learning disability • Emotional and behavioral disorders • Intellectual disability • Developmental delay • Other health impairments
GIFTED EDUCATION Underrepresentation	• Intellectual area • Academic areas (language arts, math, science, social studies) • Leadership area

THE BROKEN PIPELINE: BLACK BOYS AND TEACHER ATTITUDES

Evidence of teacher attitudes, beliefs, and practices toward African American boys is well documented in the research and theoretical literature. For example, in a qualitative study of elementary school teachers, Collier and Bush (2012) found that when teachers had negative perceptions and beliefs about African American boys, there were frequent instances of differential treatment of this population. One elementary teacher described her African American male students as "lazy, loud, having attitude problems, and not taking responsibility for their actions," and their parents as being uncaring or having low expectations for their children (p. 87). In another study, by Ferguson (2000), teachers labeled elementary school–aged African American boys as "troublemakers" and destined for jail cells.

Observations of prekindergarten and kindergarten classes found that African American boys were separated from the rest of the class and placed at desks near the teacher more often than their classmates (Barbarin & Crawford, 2006). In yet another study, Gilliam and Reyes (2016) explored the question: Are teachers implicitly biased against African American students—and African American boys in particular—as early as preschool? Their findings suggest that early childhood education teachers judge the behaviors of young children differently based on race. Gilliam and Reyes also report that teachers (White and Black) observe the behaviors of Black children, especially boys, longer when primed to detect bad behaviors. Finally, in a series of other studies, Todd, Thiem, and Neel (2016) found that images of the faces of 5-year-old Black boys were sufficient to trigger Whites into a heightened-threat mode. These studies all have one thing in common—African American boys are viewed as problems. This perception creates a climate of suspicion, fear, hyper-surveillance, and harsh punishment for children as early as 5 years of age. These examples of implicit and explicit biases, typically reserved for Black men, are generalized to young Black boys, pointing out that the system is seriously broken and that deficit thinking abounds. Schools are social institutions that adopt social ills, and this does not bode well for Black boys. As previously mentioned and corroborated by the U.S. Department of Education Office for Civil Rights (2014) and the Schott Foundation (2015), boys are extensively viewed as problems in school (Barbarin & Crawford, 2006; J. E. Davis, 2005; Losen & Gillespie, 2012; Noguera, 2008; Schott Foundation, 2015; Upchurch, 1997). Barbarin's (2013) study found that boys of color (specifically Black boys) are subjected to discrimination such as being (1) disproportionately enrolled in special education and (2) subjected to disciplinary actions, namely, suspensions and expulsions.

At the national level, which comprises approximately 16,000 school districts, Black boys' suspension rate is two to three times higher than that of White boys; and Black boys are unjustly overrepresented in special education (see U.S. Department of Education Office for Civil Rights, 2016). This overrepresentation rate is incomprehensible and beyond statistical probability. This pervasive trend is found in national, state, and district data and reports. It cannot be denied that the ways in which Black boys are socially and culturally misunderstood result in misguided school practices and thus miseducation (Woodson, 1933; Wright, Counsell, & Tate, 2015, 2016). The children, it is argued, are damaged and seen as being in need of repair rather than the schools and educators. This view absolves the educational system of its obligation to teach and reach all children.

HOW THE PIPELINE IS PRIMED: UNDERREPRESENTATION IN GIFTED EDUCATION, OVERREPRESENTATION IN DISCIPLINE AND SPECIAL EDUCATION

Of all students, Black boys have the lowest chances of being in gifted education, due mainly to under-referrals by teachers. Ford (2013) reported that Black boys' stark underrepresentation in gifted education is as high as 65% nationally, resulting in more than 125,000 Black males annually who are not receiving the education needed to reach their potential and not being provided an appropriate level of academic challenge. This problem of denied access is particularly critical for the youngest children, given that most gifted programs do not begin until grades 2–4, when many Black boys have already begun to disengage from school (Ford, Wright, Grantham, & Moore, 2017; Wright & Ford, 2017b; Wright, Ford, & Grantham, 2018; Wright, Ford, & Young, 2017). The gifts and talents of kindergartners and 1st-graders go unnurtured, begging the questions: "What are gifted Black boys doing with their gifts and talents?" "How are gifted Black boys using their gifts and talents?" Like any special need, early identification of giftedness is crucial to support students. We come back to these questions, with recommendations and resources, in Chapter 4.

In preschool, boys overall face inequitable disciplinary consequences. For example, boys are five times more likely to be expelled than girls, and Black boys are at the greatest risk for expulsion as discussed above. In fact, Black boys are suspended more than any other students, beginning in preschool. Of the school districts with children participating in preschool programs, 6% reported suspending out of school at least one preschool child. Racial disparities in out-of-school suspensions start early. This culture of excessive discipline and zero tolerance toward Black children, especially boys, perpetuates "the narrative of young Black boys requiring a tough hand to keep them in line" (Emdin, 2016, p. 5). These disproportionately high rates do not exist for any other group of males (U.S. Department of Education Office for Civil Rights, 2014).

This overrepresentation of Black boys in special education and discipline creates early childhood settings that are "oppressive places that have a primary goal of imposing rules and maintaining control" (Emdin, 2016, p. 6). As reported in Emdin's 2016 book titled *For White Folks Who Teach in the Hood . . . and the Rest of Y'all Too: Reality Pedagogy and Urban Education*, a student described "school safety" as a "nice sounding code word for treating you like you're in jail or something" (p. 6). This student's sentiment poignantly captures our next discussion point—the point of entry to the school-to-prison pipeline that stems from disciplinary practices that are harsh and discriminatory, reflecting those in the larger society.

In *Point of Entry: The Preschool-to-Prison Pipeline*, Adamu and Hogan (2015) revealed how Black students, mostly boys, are far more likely to be suspended or expelled than any other students. These disparities begin the process of pushing students out of school at very young ages, hindering their opportunities to access high-quality early education and their overall educational experiences once they enter the pre-K–12 system. Focusing on the importance of early education programs, this report emphasizes the fact that more is known about the problems than the positive development of African American boys.

Beginning in preschool, teachers have been found to stigmatize Black boys with negative labels that are passed along from teacher to teacher at each grade level. The notorious "bad boy" and "troublemaker" labels mentioned above lead to isolation and exclusion from classroom activities (Barbarin & Crawford, 2006). As a consequence, Black boys are found to be guilty by association, to be convicted without a so-called trial or hearing. The implication of such negative and stereotypical labels compromises societal expectations of Black boys; it also influences the expectations Black boys hold about themselves socially, behaviorally, psychologically, intellectually, and academically (Harper & Associates, 2014). Too frequently, Black boys do not learn to see themselves as scholars—or they unlearn doing so after being told that they are not capable of doing well with grades and behavior (Whiting, 2009). These cumulative, negative experiences result in the notion that what little Black boys are made of are "problems," "deficits," and "pathologies" rather than "possibilities," "promise," and "potential."

Mirroring the aforementioned inequities regarding disciplinary issues, special education must be addressed. The 14 special education areas—autism, deaf-blindness, deafness, developmental delay, emotional disturbance, hearing impairment, intellectual disability, multiple disabilities, orthopedic impairment, other health impairment, specific learning disability, speech or language impairment, traumatic brain injury, and visual impairment including blindness—can be placed into two categories of high and low incidence. Black boys' overrepresentation in high-incidence special education areas of developmental delay, emotional disturbance, intellectual disability, and specific learning disability is commonplace, and these areas entail greater subjectivity, engender more stigma, and require more testing (which can be culturally biased and unfair). There are also long-term and profound implications for placement and stereotypes associated with these labels. The majority of students are unjustly placed in separate classrooms and schools—also known as the most restrictive environments—which is a form of in-school segregation, both de jure and de facto. Those Black boys labeled as having emotional and behavioral disorders and intellectual disabilities have a very low probability of graduating from high school and attending college. An overwhelming number end up in the penal system (Alexander, 2010). To uncritically support views such as those espoused by Morgan et al. (2015) that Black students are in fact underrepresented and more should be identified in special education based on their "deficits" is irresponsible and egregious. We reject such views.

In contrast to these special education and disciplinary trends, creating equitable (e.g., culturally responsive) early education experiences that foster racial pride among Black boys contributes strongly to high academic achievement, including positive scholar identities, such as the view of self "as academicians, as studious, as competent and capable, and as intelligent or talented in school settings" (Whiting, 2006, p. 224), and to healthy self-identity (Wright, Counsell, & Tate, 2015, 2016). Barbarin and Crawford (2006) advise: "When African American children in general, and boys in particular, are stigmatized, it seems imperative to consider the role of race" (p. 82) in the persistent practice of assigning Black boys to low-ability classes and special education where the focus is on discipline at the expense of academics. This excessive focus on discipline in relation to Black boys highlights culturally insensitive institutional practices (e.g., zero-tolerance policies and lock-down procedures) and roadblocks that hinder the well-being of this population. To disrupt the pipeline and restore childhood innocence, more equitable and culturally responsive efforts are required that will support and nurture Black boys in developing healthy self-identities, self-esteem, social competence, academic skills, and agency in early childhood settings and beyond. These efforts must be culturally responsive and responsible as well as prevention- and intervention focused.

Against this problematic educational landscape are questions about existing practices and the quality of early education for Black boys, which is not limited to the curriculum but includes social, emotional, and psychological development. We thus present a few questions to consider regarding the quality and the sociocultural context of the early education and schooling experiences of Black boys and their overall well-being in our nation's places of learning:

1. What opportunities are missed and strengths overlooked when teachers do not know how to recognize and affirm the strengths

and potential of Black boys? This question is relevant for all teachers, regardless of their race and gender.

2. What types of culturally responsive educational experiences must be in place in the early grades to nurture the healthy development of Black boys?

3. How can educators be prepared to work effectively with Black boys?

4. How can families of Black boys—those with supports and those lacking supports—be empowered to do the best they can with what they have?

5. In essence, how do we help educators to not blame the victims and not view Black boys as "problems to be managed"?

To begin answering this last question, we need to understand that children are behind these statistics, children deserving of a high-quality education. With this in mind, we highlight what high-quality early education and care should look like overall, and specifically for Black boys, by drawing on a culturally responsive strengths-based approach.

A CULTURALLY RESPONSIVE STRENGTHS-BASED APPROACH

Taking a culturally responsive strengths-based approach focuses on what African American boys know, understand, and can do as opposed to what they cannot do or what they do not know and understand. This approach does not engage Black boys from a deficit perspective (i.e., "problems to fix"), but rather seeks to learn about the strengths, gifts, and talents of Black boys, and the best practices to leverage these strengths and assets toward school success.

This approach is informed by the theoretical and empirical work of both Gloria Ladson-Billings (2009), who coined the term *culturally responsive* or *culturally relevant* education—teaching informed by the content of the discipline and by the lives of students—and Geneva Gay (2010), who further defined culturally responsive teaching and identified its primary characteristics. We highlight these characteristics in Figure 1.2.

Given the significance, centrality, and intersection of race, gender, and social class in the schooling experiences of African American boys, it is absolutely critical that teachers understand the impact of these constructs on the overall development of young Black boys in order to ascribe to and achieve a strengths-based approach. Without a deep understanding of this intersection and its impact on Black boys, those who have been entrusted with their education and care can contribute to African American boys' development of a negative self-identity and a lack of agency to succeed in school.

Figure 1.2. Culturally Responsive Teaching Characteristics

Cultural Respect	Is demonstrated by instruction that values and acknowledges each student's knowledge base prior to entering the classroom.
Responsiveness	Describes the teacher's ability to adapt professional behaviors so that every student's knowledge and experiences are valued.
Relevance	Describes the degree to which instruction reflects students' experiences.
Rigor	Is driven by high expectations for all students through the use of exercises that are challenging and engaging.
Research	Instructional strategies and curricula should be based in strong research demonstrating effectiveness and reflecting best practice.

We assert that the knowledge discussed in this chapter and throughout this book is critical for teachers to know and understand in order to implement a culturally responsive strengths-based approach. This approach provides meaningful learning opportunities that tap the often-untapped potential of Black boys' knowledge and skills (Wright & Ford, 2017b; Wright, Young, & Ford, 2017). Because African American boys have been less likely to be exposed to culturally responsive teaching and developmentally appropriate practices associated with social, emotional, cognitive, and academic gains (LoCasale-Crouch et al., 2007), we hope that this book will contribute to changing this situation. To achieve this, we aim to help early childhood teachers create the best possible learning environments for young African American boys, environments that foster healthy self-identity and agency. This means that teachers have the knowledge, skills, and dispositions to ensure that a culturally responsive strengths-based approach is carefully designed, created, and implemented with the fidelity that honors the brilliance that we know resides in Black boys.

QUALITY EARLY EDUCATION AND CARE: AN OVERVIEW

We define high-quality early education and care for children in general, and Black boys in particular, as follows:

- Is delivered in developmentally age-appropriate classrooms and settings.
- Emphasizes social and emotional development with a culturally responsive lens.
- Stresses cognitive development, with attention to opportunity gaps and potential, while also recognizing that tests and related

evaluations of intelligence can be biased and unfair (given the long history of testing, dating several centuries) (see Gould, 1996; Naglieri & Ford, 2005, 2015).

- Utilizes high-quality, evidenced-based curriculum, with attention to ensuring that high levels of multicultural content are achieved (i.e., Banks's transformation and social action levels; see Ford, 2011).
- Has independent evaluations of classrooms, with constructive feedback and appropriate resources and supports that are culturally responsive.
- Has highly qualified teachers, who receive support to continuously become culturally competent and demonstrate such competence.
- Emphasizes culturally responsive instruction/pedagogy that is individualized through small-group and one-on-one interactions.
- Provides alignment of instruction for pre-K and K–3 to ensure seamless teaching, learning, and mastering content.
- Involves and engages parents/families in schools and provides supports at home.
- Recognizes that families have different challenges, assets, resources, and economic and cultural capital that are not distributed in equitable ways.
- Connects Black boys to gifted education, including increasing such access by creating talent development programs and activities (e.g., early intervention programs) that concentrate on rigor, high expectations, critical thinking, and problem solving. As early as possible, the gifted pipeline must be primed. As early as possible, deficit orientations (e.g., Morgan et al., 2015) must be interrogated in mindsets, research, policy, and practice.

High-quality early education and care must be culturally responsive and thus specific in support of the academic, psychological, and socioemotional development of Black boys. At a minimum, this includes:

- Instruction matched to culturally based learning styles of Black boys (as espoused by Boykin and described in Ford, 2011) while avoiding a simple "matching strategy" (discussed in greater detail in Chapter 5)
- Curriculum that is multiculturally relevant—that engages and interests Black boys
- Literature and resources that are multicultural—books, videos, materials, posters, and so forth, that reflect the racial and cultural backgrounds of Black boys
- Counseling that is multicultural and based on the development, issues, and needs of Black boys

- Tests and assessments that are fair and less discriminatory and biased against Black boys
- Teachers trained in culturally responsive classroom management, with attention to the cultural styles and practices (strengths) of Black boys
- Psychologists trained to be culturally responsive at selecting instruments and interpreting results with Black boys in mind

CONCLUSION

Black boys' experiences in education are often negative. The dismal statistics tell stories of injustice at all educational levels and in all areas of education—general education, gifted education, and special education. Disciplinary data, without questioning what is behind the numbers, can and do result in a "gloom-and-doom" reality that is bleak and without hope of change. Frustrated with the "gloom-and-doom" and deficit views of Black boys, this book is a clarion call to challenge the status quo and to offer solutions to correct these issues. This stance is long overdue in the field of early childhood where African American boys are concerned.

In this chapter, we have addressed a persistent set of issues with our focus on Black boys at the initial stages of their formal educational lives and how these are shaped by deficit views out in the world and in schools on the part of those who have been entrusted with their education and care. Our focus is on building racial and cultural competence in the early childhood classroom so that all children, Black boys in particular, can thrive. We seek to support Black boys early in their lives and disrupt the many problems that virtually guarantee that they will not experience academic and social success. There are no quick fixes, but change is possible. Change is essential. Too much is at stake when we fail to and are afraid to answer the timeless question, "What are little [Black] boys made of?"

CHAPTER 2

Early Childhood Experiences of Black Boys in School

"Karl Is Ready. Are You?"

Karl—bright, inquisitive, vibrant, and full of possibilities—was born in 2011 and entered kindergarten in 2016 ready to learn and explore the four Rs: reading, writing, arithmetic, and race. At the age of 4, he is academically and cognitively advanced. He has an extensive vocabulary (most people think he is 6 or 7 years old), is advanced in math, including adding and subtracting in his head (without counting on fingers). Karl can count past 100 and knows all letters of the alphabet (upper and lower case), spells his name, knows all colors (primary, secondary, and tertiary). He loves books and demands that his family read to him. Karl is more than ready for school. Also important to note is that Karl speaks openly about skin color. Thus, he is academically and culturally advanced. When playing a video game with family, he was asked to choose his character. Karl chose the darkest shade, yet his skin tone is light (a caramel shade). His family was pleased to see this Black boy recognizing skin color and doing so in a positive and prideful way. What would teachers (the majority of whom are White) have said or done—if anything? Are they comfortable talking about race with young children? Are they competent at doing so? What resources will they use? Will Karl encounter expectations that are at odds with his social-cultural development? (Wright, Ford, & Walters, 2016, p. 81)

What will become of the Karls of the world is a question that occupies the first author's thoughts each morning on his drive to work at a local university in the Mid-South where both authors prepare primarily White, working-class and middle-class female teacher candidates (mirroring the national demographic) to teach all children, but especially Black boys (see McFarland et al., 2017; Sleeter & Milner, 2011).

As one approaches the final stretch of the drive to the university along a tree-lined avenue, there is a billboard that displays an advertisement for a local private school. The school's tuition rivals that of local colleges and universities in and around the city, state, and the nation, for that matter. The billboard's display is a White boy with blond hair and blue eyes who looks about 7 or 8 years of age. Accentuated by very large letters is the phrase "We Know Boys." Below the image are the words "Building Better Boys." The striking image of the little boy superimposed on the billboard gives the impression that it is worth envisioning a bright future for this boy, with his cheerful smile and preppy style of dress, a future that begins with a supportive learning environment that values and recognizes his strengths and needs, and also integrates his sociocultural experiences. Moreover, it is worth structuring opportunities for optimal learning that places his self-identity at the center of pedagogy to ensure that his interests are foregrounded. This is the privileged (and taken-for-granted) reality for countless White, middle-class children.

These students enter schools that reflect, represent, and enforce their "ways with words" (Heath, 1983) and their ways of organizing their experiences (physical development) and expressing meaning (cognitive and socioemotional development) through the major domains of child/human development. Unfortunately, this is not the reality of schooling, teaching, and learning for children of color in general, African American children in particular, and Black boys especially.

PRESCHOOL EDUCATION

The National Institute for Early Education Research (Barnett et al., 2010) reports that some children of color, particularly Black preschoolers, are the least likely to gain access to high-quality early care and education. Barnett, Carolan, and Johns (2013), using results from the National Center for Education Statistics study of observational ratings of preschool settings, reported that although 40% of Hispanic and 36% of White children were enrolled in center-based classrooms rated as "high," only 25% of Black children were in classrooms with the same rating. Furthermore, 15% of Black children attended child-care centers ranked as "low"—almost twice the percentage of Hispanic and White children. Hispanic and Black children in home-based settings were even worse off, with over 50% in settings rated as low compared with only 30% for White children (Dobbins, McCready, & Rackas, 2016).

Complicating matters further is the reality that Black children face a myriad of structural obstacles where the odds seem to be stacked against their success (Barbarin, Murry, Tolan, & Graham, 2016). For instance, African American boys are disproportionately excluded from meaningful educational opportunities in part because inexperienced teachers lack familiarity with their cultural repertoires (e.g., Boykin, 1994, as discussed in Chapter 5). This exclusion is exacerbated by the stigmatization of African American boys as "bad" boys (Barbarin & Crawford, 2006). Sadly, even the classmates of these boys learn early to associate the labels and messages of "bad" and "troublemaker" with African American boys, which perpetuates a climate of suspicion and fear that spirals into school "discipline hubs" for Black boys.

SCHOOL "DISCIPLINE HUBS" AND BLACK BOYS

The fact that this labeling begins in preschool and continues through high school has contributed to the overzealous application of zero-tolerance policies and practices that largely discriminate against Black (and Brown) boys, thus exacerbating the school-to-prison pipeline (Allen & White-Smith, 2015; Bryan, 2017; Losen, 2013; Wright & Ford, 2016a). Consequently, rather than in classrooms of optimal learning and development, where the potential, promise, and possibilities of African American boys' success can be nurtured and cultivated, they find themselves in what appear to be school "discipline hubs" where the focus is extensively about maintaining order. These discipline hubs often utilize "quasi-military" tactics in which students (1) wear identical school uniforms; (2) walk in straight/orderly lines (facing forward, arms beside their person); and (3) do not talk (speaking only when spoken to with the referent "Yes, sir!" when appropriate). All of this occurs under the direction and supervision of a teacher (usually male) firmly articulating rigid expectations and instructions. This dystopian approach to disciplining African American boys runs counter to more progressive methods, such as restorative justice, which emphasize authentic dialogue, mutual understanding, and communal responsibility (Fergus, Noguera, & Martin, 2014).

This focus on discipline under the guise of supporting social–emotional development is often at the expense of fostering a healthy self-identity and agency in African American boys. When Black boys experience schooling environments where they are not recognized for their strengths and not understood in terms of their needs (which are not necessarily weaknesses), and where their identities are criminalized, adultified, and ignored, they learn the message early that schools do not support, encourage, and care for their overall humanity and development. Consequently, this hyper-focus on discipline begins the "prepping process" that funnels African American boys out of school and into the prison industrial complex (Bryan, 2017; Schott Foundation, 2012; Wright & Ford, 2016a).

Additional evidence of this preoccupation and hyper-focus on discipline is documented in the report *2013–2014 Civil Rights Data Collection: A First Look* (U.S. Department of Education Office for Civil Rights, 2016). The report is a survey of all public schools and school districts in the United States and focuses on a number of variables, including school discipline, special education, and gifted education. The findings reveal that African American children, specifically boys, are suspended from school at an overwhelmingly high rate. For example, as mentioned previously, Black preschool children are 3.6 times as likely to receive one or more out-of-school suspensions as White preschool children. Moreover, while Black boys represent only 19% of the preschool enrollment, they represent 45% of preschool children receiving one or more out-of-school suspensions. Conversely, White children, who represent 41% of preschool enrollment, account for only 28% of preschool children receiving one or more out-of-school suspensions (U.S. Department of Education Office for Civil Rights, 2016). These alarming statistics raise the question, "Do we know boys, specifically Black boys, beyond the repeated criminalization and adultification of their behaviors?"

BLACK BOYS: A CLOSER LOOK

Research shows that, all too often, boys are viewed as problems in school (Barbarin & Crawford, 2006; Dancy, 2014; Ferguson, 2000; Hotchkins, 2016; T. C. Howard, 2014; Ladson-Billings, 2011; Toldson & Johns, 2016; Warren, 2016; Wright & Ford, 2016c). In a study spanning the primary school years, Barbarin (2013) found that boys of color (specifically African American boys) are subject to disproportionately high rates of disciplinary action, such as suspensions and expulsions. These actions, combined with the ways that Black boys are socially and culturally misunderstood, result in misguided school practices that disadvantage them in punitive ways (Wright, Counsell, & Tate, 2015).

As the Office for Civil Rights data highlighted above reveal, preschool boys are five times more likely to be expelled than girls, and African American boys are most at risk for expulsion. The question is why. Beginning in preschool, some teachers stigmatize African American boys, giving them labels, such as "bad boy" or "troublemaker," that are a manifestation of prevailing stereotypes of Black boys as criminal, deviant, lazy, rebellious, lacking potential, and anti-intellectual. Over time—and it happens relatively quickly—the impact of these labels affects societal expectations of African American boys and at times the expectations they have for themselves—socially, academically, and vocationally (Harper & Associates, 2014).

Much like school discipline practices, there are similar trends found in the rates of African American boys recommended for emotional support services (Irving & Hudley, 2008) and being labeled as having serious emotional disturbances (Holzman, 2006). What does not seem coincidental is the fact that 70% of African American boys identified as having a disability have also been suspended (Losen & Gillespie, 2012). The implications of the high rates of suspension and expulsion, combined with the practice of disproportionately referring African American boys for special education, contribute significantly to their presumed dysfunction. These implications also reify and reinforce negative and often unexamined narratives about the social and academic promise, potential, possibility—not to mention the humanity—of this population. These deficit views and the indictment of the identities of Black boys are a reminder that we do not know all boys. Even educators who have been entrusted with their education and care cannot completely know all boys.

BLACK BOYS AND TEACHER ATTITUDES

This familiar practice of "blaming the victim" downplays and minimizes the role of teacher attitudes, beliefs, and practices and how these manifest in negative interactions with African American boys. Moreover, blaming the victim ignores the web of institutional and systemic oppression that literally surrounds African American boys beginning in preschool (Wright, Counsell, & Tate, 2015). These ignored factors and unexamined structural inequalities serve to subvert the development of a healthy self-identity and school success of African American boys. This suppresses and represses the establishment in those early years of a "resilient personality and cognitive structures which will be the foundation of the child's future personal, cognitive, social style" (A. N. Wilson, 1978, p. 71).

Evidence of teachers' deficit-oriented attitudes, beliefs, and practices toward non-White students in general, and African American boys in particular, is well documented in the research literature and has been presented in Chapter 1. However, we return to teacher attitudes and the implications for teacher preparation in part because, as Nieto (2005) pointed out:

> It is no surprise that some teachers have negative perceptions, biases, and racist attitudes about the students they teach, and about the students' families, cultures, and communications. . . . Teachers . . . pick up the same messages and misconceptions that we all do, and it is only by confronting the ones that get in the way of student learning that change will occur. This means encouraging prospective and practicing teachers to reflect deeply on their beliefs and attitudes . . . [and providing] them with the resources and support they need for doing this kind of difficult but, in the long run, empowering work. (pp. 217–218)

This quote is a reminder of the importance of teacher education programs being intentional about the opportunities they provide teacher candidates through critical coursework and field experiences in a variety of settings (e.g., urban) with diverse students. At the heart of their coursework and experiences out in the field must be opportunities to "become aware that their expectations of [their future] students are affected by the ways they have been socialized as individuals and teachers" (Ryan, 2006, p. 11). We argue that these experiences have the potential to contribute to teacher candidates' capacity to understand that their ability to be effective with "other people's children" (Delpit, 1995, 2006) lies in their deep understanding of the personal and cultural identities of their students.

Implications for Teacher Education

The implications for teacher education programs that continue to be homogeneous (i.e., dominated by White students and professors) demand that teacher candidates be routinely exposed to coursework and field experiences with students from culturally, linguistically, and economically diverse backgrounds in order to critically explore the connections between racial and ethnic identities and pedagogy (T. C. Howard, 2010; Lee, 2007; Nieto, 2010). This is absolutely necessary given that teacher candidates are expected to teach students, in this case Black boys, who come from different backgrounds with varying life experiences that may not be familiar to the candidates.

The need to bridge cultural knowledge and pedagogy (Lee, 2007) in teacher education is of critical importance when working with Black boys. We have found in our work with teacher candidates that this need is equally important for those teachers who share the racial and ethnic backgrounds of their students. As discussed in Chapter 3, it cannot be assumed that because teachers match with their students in terms of racial or ethnic backgrounds, they can easily translate cultural knowledge into culturally relevant teaching without a deep awareness of the many cultures their students represent and how these might affect their teaching and their students' learning.

For decades, the underrepresentation of African, Asian, Hispanic, and Native Americans in teacher education programs and among teacher educators, as well as among teachers in pre-K–12 schools, has not been a match with student diversity. While student diversity has continued to increase, teacher diversity has not. Some 52% of students are non-White, but some 85% of teachers are White (Kena et al., 2016). Based on these statistics, the likelihood that a Black boy (or girl) will encounter a teacher who looks like him or her is slim. The likelihood of cultural clashes, however, is far greater when teachers fail to see strengths and gifts in non-White students in general, and Black boys in particular (Wright, Ford, & Grantham, 2018). The implications of this demographic reality as it relates to Black boys are captured in the classroom observation described below, which demonstrates the impact of teacher attitudes on the schooling experience of a Black boy named Joshua.

My Name Is Joshua

Consider a detailed observation conducted by Bryan (2017), a university supervisor of preservice teacher candidates at a predominantly White institution in the South. He recalls a troubling observation of a Black boy named Joshua in a 3rd-grade classroom with his White female mentor teacher, a White female student teacher, and a White female classmate. In a conversation with Bryan, Mrs. Kay (the mentor teacher) informed him that Joshua recently transferred from a "low-performing" urban school and was not academically prepared for the rigor of his new school. According to Bryan (2017), Mrs. Kay's deficit thinking of Joshua as "failing miserably," "a behavioral problem," "different," and "uncomfortable" (p. 328) influenced how the student teacher (22-year-old Chelsea) perceived and interacted with Joshua.

The observation continued with the student teacher taking the entire class to the school's media center. It is a common practice in schools for young children to move from place to place in a line. Likewise, it is to be expected that, on occasion, some children may get out of the line. This was the case for several White boys, prompting the student teacher to gently remind them to stay in line. However, the same approach was not taken with Joshua, who, several minutes later, was out of line, albeit for a brief moment. Once the student teacher noticed he was out of line, she immediately scolded him: "Get back in line, Joshua! Didn't you hear me when I told everyone to remain in line?" (Bryan, 2017, p. 328). Immediately following this reprimand, Emma Kay (classmate), who was standing in front of Joshua in line, said to him, using the same harsh tone of voice to imitate the student teacher, "Get back in line and stay there!" (p. 329). Joshua, on the verge of tears, suddenly found himself at odds with the student teacher and his classmate. In an instant, the deficit views of Joshua that began with Mrs. Kay resulted in a ripple effect that led to the perpetuation of an "intergenerational lineage and socialization about Black boys" (p. 329), including, but not limited to, deficit messages, biases, and stereotypes that were passed down from the mentor teacher, to the student teacher, to the classmate. This treatment of Black boys that White children as well as student teachers are witnessing in schools can have a deleterious effect on how Black boys construct and maintain a healthy self-identity and a sense of agency in the early grades.

These studies all have in common the theme that teachers and classmates of African American boys view them as problems. To reiterate, these views create an uncomfortable climate of suspicion, fear, hyper-surveillance, and harsh punishment. These examples of implicit bias, racism, and discrimination typically reserved for Black men in society are generalized to Black boys sometimes as early as preschool. This points to the importance of building racial and cultural competence in teachers, which requires exposure to accurate historical and contemporary knowledge and understandings about non-White groups, so that they can develop culturally responsive and responsible skills to effectively teach culturally diverse students.

As noted by Barbarin and Crawford (2006), "When African American children in general, and boys in particular, are stigmatized, it seems imperative to consider the role of race" (p. 82). This brings us to why it is important to rethink school readiness for Black boys. By this, we mean that school officials (administrators and teachers) must learn how to recognize, understand, and engage the kinds of talk, thinking, and "everyday" experiences that Black boys bring to the early childhood classroom from their homes and communities. This is absolutely critical to their school success in light of the unique challenges and the complex ways in which structural and systemic racism and discrimination in schools and society shape the experiences and social–emotional development of Black boys.

In the sections that follow, we discuss rethinking school readiness and the importance of valuing the everyday language of African American boys, and we conclude with how these out-of-school experiences have the potential to map onto the development of science, technology, engineering, and mathematics (STEM) identities.

RETHINKING SCHOOL READINESS (FOR WHOM? AND FOR WHAT?)

Given that school readiness is considered a strong predictor of later academic outcomes, there are far too many reports that fail to adequately address the root cause of why so many African American boys (the Karls and Joshuas of the world) encounter teachers (Mrs. Kay and Chelsea) who perceive them to be unprepared for school. These stubborn and ubiquitous deficit views demand a thoughtful and thorough revision of school readiness (see Wright, Ford, & Walters, 2016) toward a strengths-based and asset-based approach that recognizes, understands, and integrates the language, culture, and family frames of reference and social–emotional practices that African American boys bring to their schooling experience. Supporting the school readiness and success of African American boys demands that their teachers take an anti-deficit view that values versus devalues the funds of knowledge, skills, and dispositions of this population. Recognizing, understanding, valuing, and integrating the ways of knowing, talking, and interacting that African American boys demonstrate in early childhood classrooms are critical if teachers are going to be ready for the inquisitive and vibrant Karls of the world instead of silencing the Joshuas of the world.

Statistics have a way of dehumanizing the lives and experiences of children from nondominant and historically marginalized groups, and there is no shortage of reports on Black boys in pre-K–12 indicating a prevalence of deficit thinking about their academic readiness. This misguided thinking is further supported by the perceived absence of simple skills on the part of Black boys, like remembering to raise a hand to be recognized to speak, following directions, completing tasks, and not staying in line (as in Joshua's case and many like his). Consequently, failure to complete tasks believed to demonstrate school readiness prevents an alarming number of African American boys from engaging in the learning process. For example, the U.S. Department of Education Office of Civil Rights 2015 task force report indicates that 71% of White children entering kindergarten can recognize letters, compared with 57% of African American children. Relatedly, more than 140,000 kindergarten students nationwide were held back a year during the 2013–2014 school year, representing about 4% of all kindergarten students in public schools. Native Hawaiian, other Pacific Islander, American Indian, and Native Alaskan students are held back each year at nearly twice the rate of White children. The significance of these retention data may lie in the need for school officials to rethink school readiness in terms of its purpose, its target, and the conditions under which it is encountered. It is reasonable to assert that many Black boys are ready for school, but school is not ready for them (see Webb-Johnson, 2002).

These retention data highlight the critical need for teachers to work responsively and responsibly from a cultural lens, in support of the school readiness and success of and for African American boys. The implications of understanding these data are significant and raise an important question regarding what is really preventing such a sizable number of African American boys from being fully engaged in the learning process. Is it simply failure to demonstrate the requisite social skills, or are other factors (e.g., race and gender) also at work? We believe it is the latter and that it begins with teachers and administrators lacking familiarity with African American children's "ways with words" (Heath, 1983)—their ways of sharing and expressing meaning based largely on their everyday concrete, familiar, commonplace, and informal experiences. In many early childhood classrooms, these ways of sharing and expressing are viewed as maladaptive instead of adaptive. For example, the concept of *verve* is characterized by three components: (1) lively and intensified behavior, (2) preference for variety and alternations within a given setting, and (3) preference for multiple background elements existing simultaneously in one's environment, including activities and stimulation (Boykin et al., 2005; Williams, 2015).

Research has focused on the characteristic of verve (i.e., variability) and its value in the home environments of many African American children (Boykin 1983, 2001; Boykin & Bailey, 2000; Hale, 1982; Tyler, Boykin, & Walton, 2006). And yet, within teacher preparation programs, scholarly readings and in-class activities based on Boykin's model are largely absent as important knowledge that teacher candidates should possess. As a result, schools and classrooms remain places and spaces that are not culturally responsive or neutral for Black children, and boys in particular (Delpit, 2006; Gay, 2010; Wright & Ford, 2016a; Wright, Ford, & Walters, 2016). When Black boys display vervistic behaviors in the early childhood classroom, teachers will see students with high levels of energy, who are easily excited, physically active when engaged and mentally stimulated, and "loud" when excited or engaged. Such behaviors are perceived (or, as we argue, misperceived) by teachers as not appropriate and in opposition to traditional ways of learning. Challenging the latter view, we invite teachers to reconsider their often-negative perceptions of classroom behaviors of Black boys from a position of strengths and assets versus deficits.

What can be gleaned from an understanding of verve in early childhood settings is the relevance of culture in teaching, learning, and schooling. When teaching practices build on cultural practices, such as vervistic behaviors that many Black boys bring to their learning, their social and academic outcomes are enhanced because their cognitive, academic, psychological, physical, and sociocultural backgrounds are integrated and valued in classrooms. When teachers create learning environments that include multiple classroom activities and lend themselves to high levels of energy, this provides many, but not all, Black boys with ways of expressing themselves through their everyday ways of knowing and being, which are not based on their ability to approximate White, middle-class standards of academic achievement and social competencies (Delpit, 1995).

As we move on with recommendations for valuing the everyday language practices of Black boys, we offer examples of how to move from cultural clashes with school readiness to culturally responsive strengths-based practices, depicted in Figure 2.1.

VALUING "EVERYDAY" LANGUAGE PRACTICES

We begin this section with a story cited in Dandy's (1991) book titled *Black Communications: Breaking Down the Barriers* in which she recalls an observation conducted as a graduate assistant supervising undergraduate teacher education majors. During this particular observation, Dandy witnessed what she described as a rejection of a child's dialect rendering. She observed Joey, a lively and intelligent 3rd-grade African American boy who was in the highest reading group, and Alice, a White female student teacher who had been preparing for an entire week to teach this high-performing group of young readers. During the observation, Joey was excited and eager to sit next to Alice in hopes that he would be called on to read first. He was eager to share his stellar reading skills. To introduce the story, Alice posed the question, "Have you ever felt as if nobody loved you?" (p. 2). Several students recalled a time when they felt like an outsider. Still excited, Joey could not wait to be called on to read. He soon got his wish as Alice asked him to read. With confidence, Joey began to read:

> "Maxie. Maxie lived in three small rooms on the top floor of an old brownstone house on Orange Skreet.
> "She . . ."
> "Not skreet, Joey. Say street."
> "Skreet."
> "Read the sentence again." (p. 2)

Figure 2.1. From Cultural Clashes with School Readiness to a Culturally Responsive Strengths-Based Practices Approach

School Readiness	African American Culture	Culturally Responsive Recommendations
Sit quietly	Movement oriented and vervistic (May be considered immature and lacking self-control)	Encourage indoor and outdoor large-motor and whole-body experiences, such as putting mats in spacious areas to encourage boys (and girls) to tumble and roll
Follow rules	Expressive individualism—creative, risk taker (May be considered defiant and disrespectful)	Create opportunities for spontaneous and continuous exploration of "What if . . . ?" questions
Draw within the lines	Expressive individualism—creative, imaginative, thinks outside the box (May be viewed as lacking manual dexterity, having delayed fine-motor skills, and immature)	Observe closely with a strengths-based lens and note three things that you noticed that you may not have seen previously
Know first and last name	Expressive individualism—likes to make up names, including nicknames (May be viewed as immature, having a learning disability, or unintelligent)	Support children's initiative and curiosity about their own interests and the world around them
Listen when others talk, especially teacher	Oral tradition—call and response (May be viewed as rude and disrespectful)	Use cultural strengths, such as oral traditions in African American communities, to develop emergent reading and writing skills
Do not question or challenge authority figures	Oral tradition—blunt and direct (May be viewed as rude and a bad or troubled child)	Acknowledge the legitimacy of cultural heritages as legacies that affect children's dispositions and attitudes and are worthy curriculum content
Are quiet when working	Oral tradition—enjoys talking and expressing self in all contexts (May talk during all assignments, even assessments)	Think about the early learning environment and how it meets needs and reflects strengths
Are independent	Communal—interdependent, social, and extroverted (May be perceived as lacking independence)	Consider what strengths appear and how can they be leveraged
Share	Communal—strong affiliation to loved ones first (May not share with those they don't trust)	Be explicit about respecting diverse cultures, experiences, and practices
Take responsibility	Communal—protective of friends and loved ones (May get in trouble helping and taking up for others)	Use the home culture and learning as a positive platform on which to build learning

Adapted from Wright, Ford, & Walters (2016).

Rereading the sentence, Joey continued to pronounce *skreet* instead of *street*. Frustrated with Joey's pronunciation of *street*, in front of the entire class Alice reread the sentence and then asked Joey to continue with the next line in the story. Feeling embarrassed, Joey proceeded with caution: "Every morning at exactly 7:10, Maxie's large orange cat jumped onto the middle window sill and skretched out . . ." (p. 2). Alice responded, "No, Joey. You are doing it again. Say 'stretched.'" In a muffled tone, Joey pronounced "skretched" again. With his confidence shaken, his view of himself as an advanced reader now suspect, Joey did not read any more of the story.

Consider the impact of Alice's pedagogical approach. Alice was a seemingly well-meaning student teacher who wanted to ensure that students pronounced words correctly. Alice's focus on correct pronunciation was at the expense of the importance of reading for meaning. Unfortunately, it was also at the expense of Joey's identity as a learner in general, and a reader in particular.

Joey's use of language raises questions regarding the treatment of children's home cultures, especially non-White children, in the curriculum and classroom. Another question that this observation raises is whether Alice learned about dialects, vernaculars, and "everyday" language practices and how they manifest both in and outside of the classroom. Had Alice been taught in her teacher preparation program that the best way to learn "standard English" was to reject all other varieties in favor of school-based and discipline-based ways of talking, acting, and knowing? A more important question is: What are the short-term and long-term effects of this rejection of Joey's language use on his growth and development as learner and reader?

When consideration is given to the short-term and long-term effects on Joey's identity as a learner, it is critical to focus on the importance of preparing culturally competent preservice teachers to recognize, understand, and value home and cultural out-of-school practices (e.g., ways of talking, acting, and knowing) that African American boys bring to their schooling. This recognition is meant to honor "the child's home discourse as a rich source of knowledge and learning itself" (Ballenger, 1999, p. 6). Integrating the academic experiences of African American boys early in their schooling in authentic, positive, and culturally responsive ways supports their school readiness and overall school success.

This valuing of everyday language practices, when recognized, understood, and integrated into the curriculum, prepares students like Joey for positive learner outcomes (see Delpit & Dowdy, 2002; Kinloch, 2012; Kirkland, 2013; Paris, 2012). This type of affirmation, in early childhood learning environments, provides support for school readiness and success of African American boys while at the same time helping teachers to recognize the "linguistic, literate, and cultural practices many students of color [bring] from their homes and communities" (Paris, 2012, p. 93) as strengths and not deficits. The latter is achieved when real value is placed on children's home cultures and when strategic attempts are made to determine how these "ways with words" can be transferred to the school environment, thereby making learning relevant by connecting teachers to the expressive ways of talking, acting, and knowing of African American boys, as well as their ability to reason, problem solve, and draw from their cultural resources to construct personal meaning out of their schooling experience. We now turn to STEM, where we find that African American boys' ways of talking, acting, and knowing are suspect even in the literature focused on STEM education.

BLACK BOYS AND STEM

While young children (aged 3–8 years) have the capacity to engage in STEM investigations, schools and educators consistently underestimate children's abilities in general (National Research Council, 2007). Low expectations for STEM outcomes are further complicated and hindered by stereotypes and assumptions about STEM learning aptitudes assigned to young children representing various nondominant groups such as African American boys (Wright, 2011b, 2011c; Wright & Ford, 2017a). For instance, in STEM research by Rosebery and Warren (2001), they explained:

> The talk of an African-American child who conveys his ideas about science in the form of a story is often seen by educators who operate with majority, "mainstream" perspectives as somehow less "scientific" or "mathematical" than the talk of a white child who conveys her ideas in objective, propositional language. (p. 4)

As a result of the "White folks' pedagogy" (Emdin, 2016, p. ix) and racialized and gendered narratives about Black children, boys especially are presumed to lack intelligence when it comes to academics, particularly in science and math. The result of this is early childhood and primary-grade teachers missing the daily opportunities to engage all young children in STEM activities that promote scientific thinking, mathematical reasoning, and engineering design in general (Counsell, Peat, Vaughan, & Johnson, 2015; Wright, 2011b; Wright, Counsell, Goings, Freeman, & Peat , 2016).

These negative messages downplay and minimize the reasoning and sense-making (e.g., experiences, knowledge, beliefs) resources that African American boys use as they engage in STEM learning. These low expectations of African American boys obfuscate their academic talent and further discourage their development of identities in STEM. When the latter happens, the windows of early learning and development, long believed to exist for language acquisition and mathematical concepts and now extended to scientific thinking, leave the participation of Black boys far behind. This untapped potential contributes to later STEM disparities. For example, in 2011, Blacks received just 6% of all STEM bachelor's degrees and less than half of those were awarded to Black males. Overall, Blacks received 4% of master's degrees and 2% of PhDs in STEM, despite constituting 12% of the U.S. population (McGee, 2015).

The aforementioned disparities raise questions regarding what is needed to create access and opportunity to prepare African American boys for STEM trajectories in pre-K–12. Moreover, what opportunities are missed when teachers do not know how to see the strengths in the talk and reasoning of Black boys? How do we build on those out-of-school experiences that Black boys deploy in the early childhood education classroom as having real value in the STEM classroom?

An example of a teacher purposefully seeing the strengths in the talk and reasoning of Black boys is captured in an observation that describes Steve, an African American boy considered to be a rambunctious 1st-grader, who asks a lot of questions and makes comments as an active participant during the reading of science information books. Steve and his classmates participate in a unit about plants where they explore the insides of pumpkins by "digging their hands inside to pull out the pulp and seeds. They smell and feel the pulp, take out and count the seeds, describe the pumpkin's characteristics in their journals" (Varelas, Martin, & Kane, 2013, as cited in Schroeder, n.d., p. 2). The teacher invites students to gather on the rug to discuss their findings. Steve explains his experience of pulling a handful of pulp out of a pumpkin by declaring, "something was growing in my hands" (Varelas et al., 2013, as cited in Schroeder, n.d., p. 2). His declaration does not go unnoticed by his teacher, Ms. G, who immediately uses Steve's statement as a way to encourage a rich discussion. This dialogic, inquiry-based approach acknowledges Steve's reasoning and "ways with words," giving him access to teaching and learning in ways that support his sharing of ideas, asking of questions, and making connections to his own experiences. Martin and Varelas comment:

> The fact that this boy is both African American and a scientist are critically important. Too often, these identities are viewed as incompatible, shunting African American children and their competencies in very narrow and limited ways. (as cited in Schroeder, n.d., p. 2)

Martin and Varelas also express concern over the continued framing of African American children from the position of the racial achievement gap, which ignores opportunity gaps and implies that African American children are less capable than their peers in math and science, based mainly on test scores. They further argue that test scores "have little capacity to measure the true growth as a scientist of this precocious boy with pumpkin smeared all over his hands" (Martin & Varelas, as cited in Schroeder, n.d., p. 2).

To assist teachers in recognizing those opportunity gaps in order to provide greater access, Varelas and colleagues (2013) developed a teaching, learning, and research framework for content learning (CL) and identity construction (IC). Their CLIC framework focuses on three intersecting identities: *disciplinary* identity (as doers of the discipline such as mathematics and science), *racial* identity (emerging understandings of what it means to be Black), and *academic* identity (as participants in academic tasks and classroom practices). Although this framework has been used largely in elementary and middle school science and mathematics classrooms, its usefulness in early childhood classrooms is worth exploring.

In addition to considering the CLIC framework in the early childhood STEM classroom to understand how Black boys negotiate participation in and come to see themselves as doers of STEM, we recommend critical child development theories, ECE pedagogy (e.g., inquiry teaching, project-based learning), and/or culturally responsive curriculum models, as discussed in greater detail in Chapter 5.

CONCLUSION

To know boys is not enough. We must consider the school experiences of Karl, Joshua, Joey, Steve, and other African American boys as "oppressive [and repressive] places that have a primary goal of imposing rules and maintaining control" (Emdin, 2016, p. 6) at the expense of authentic and responsive learning. Supporting African American boys' school readiness and academic success requires that school officials (administrators and teachers) have deep understandings of how Black boys negotiate and navigate their schooling context. To achieve these goals, objectives, and aims, early childhood education teacher preparation programs in particular must educate their majority White female teacher candidates on the importance of integrating anti-bias curriculum (see Derman-Sparks & Edwards, 2010; York, 2016), multicultural education (see Ramsey, 2015), culturally responsive teaching (see Ladson-Billings, 2009; Gay, 2010), and social justice (Banks, 2009) into their future classrooms. Such practices are meaningless, however, if teachers have not critically examined their own attitudes, beliefs, and values, and how these manifest in teaching, learning, and schooling. It is important to note here that "it is possible for people of all racial and ethnic backgrounds to take on approaches to teaching that hurt youth of color" (Emdin, 2016, p. viii). In other words, skin color does not necessarily equal consciousness.

The challenge is not simply to ensure that this is done in a manner pedagogically sound and relevant to the students' needs. Rather, teachers must receive intentional training and preparation that focus on intersectionality, which is the systematic study of the ways in which differences, such as race, gender, class, ethnicity, and other sociopolitical and cultural identities, interrelate and inform and shape teaching, learning, and schooling. They must be encouraged and supported in their efforts to embrace such practices in their daily planning of lessons and activities, instructional delivery, and management of the multicultural/multi-ethnic classroom climate (Wright, Ford, & Walters, 2016). This way of teaching also requires accountability; that is, someone (e.g., a cultural competence coach) must oversee the work that is being done to effect culturally responsive changes.

Without attention to intersectionality that is grounded in the approaches mentioned above and frequent opportunities for teacher candidates to interrogate their attitudes and beliefs about "other people's children" (see Delpit, 2006), there is a risk that teachers' beliefs about African American boys will give way to unexamined assumptions. Such deficit-based assumptions, taken to be "truths," serve as justification for blaming Black boys and their families for their "relative lack . . . [while] ignoring the myriad of strengths and tremendous resilience that exist" (Nasir, 2012, p. 2) among these students and their families.

When racial disproportionality in school discipline begins as early as preschool (due largely to unfavorable attitudes and beliefs about African American boys), implicit bias, racism, and discrimination are heavily implicated, with consequences that severely impact the educational experiences and life outcomes of this population. This occurs long before African American boys have had an opportunity to demonstrate their promise, potential, and possibility. African American boys who enter school eager and enthusiastic to learn, begin to feel unwanted and out of place. These feelings early on turn to disengagement from the school context, exacerbated by harsh punishment and classroom isolation that leaves them vulnerable to stereotypes and ongoing discrimination (Barbarin & Crawford, 2006; Fergus, Noguera, & Martin, 2014; Sprung, Froschl, & Gropper, 2010; Wright et al., 2015). The manifestation of early disengagement is reflected in the decline in African American boys' test scores by 4th grade, assignment to low-ability groups in reading and math, denied access to gifted education, and an increase in special education referrals (Wright et al., 2016a).

In contrast to these disciplinary and special education trends is the need to create equitable (e.g., culturally responsive) early education and care experiences that foster healthy racial identities among African American boys that contribute strongly to high academic achievement—a scholar identity (Whiting, 2009; Wright et al., 2015). This anti-deficit view sees the promise, potential, and possibilities with regard to African American boys' ways with words, reasoning skills, and interactional styles. Ultimately, the narrative of Black boys will turn from "impossible" to "I'm possible." As educational professionals responsible for impressionable young children, we must believe this.

CHAPTER 3

Creating a Culture of Success

This Little Light of Mine . . .

An African American family of five (including two daughters and one son) recently moved to a new state and, therefore, a new school district. The parents were deliberate about choosing this community and school—a higher-income and racially diverse suburb of a major urban area in the Southeast. All of the children earn high grades, seldom less than a B; the oldest has been identified as gifted since 3rd grade; the middle child was referred for gifted screening in the former school and is being assessed at the current school; and their son, Keith, shows signs of giftedness but the program does not begin until 3rd grade. Keith's teacher (an African American female) often sends home negative reports regarding his behavior, reporting that he is a follower and easily distracted (i.e., daydreams and is off task). The parents are strict disciplinarians, both having grown up in the military as children, and the father is retired from the service. His style is authoritarian. The mother vacillates between authoritarian and authoritative. When grades drop and behavior is a problem, she is no-nonsense. This mother sees great potential in her children and will not accept less than their best effort and work ethic. Keith's class was attending a field trip but his parents decided that he would not go due to poor behavior reported by his teacher. At the end of the school day, the teacher sent the mother an email message to say that Keith had misbehaved twice during the field trip and would be attending in-school suspension. How is this possible given that he was not at school or on the field trip? The parents must intervene before the light dims for this African American boy in terms of motivation, engagement, and self-image as a learner. (Adapted from Wright & Ford, 2016a)

The title of this vignette, taken from the Negro spiritual "This Little Light of Mine," captures the hopes and dreams of a Black family whose desire is for their children to be successful in school. In light of the previous chapters, holding fast to their hopes and dreams for all of their children, especially their son Keith, can be difficult in the face of the onslaught of negative attitudes and beliefs that persist about Black boys. Navigating institutionalized inequity, injustice, marginalization, and oppression based on, and justified by, racist ideology that views Black boys as less innocent and childlike than their White counterparts is psychologically and physically exhausting. While other families not raising a Black boy have the luxury of worrying about normative child developmental milestones and experiences, Black families find themselves holding vigil to ensure the light (promise, potential, and possibility) of their son does not dim or, worse, is not extinguished long before it has an opportunity to shine. As will be discussed and confronted head-on in this chapter, there is a clear and undeniable impact of teachers who operate from and with a racist ideology on the development of identity, voice, and agency of Black boys, as illustrated in the vignette above.

As long as public schools continue to manifest racist and discriminatory practices resulting from unchallenged attitudes, beliefs, and practices, ongoing deficits, disparities, and gaps in educational achievement (and life outcomes) will remain. Moreover, the call for change issued by the National Association for the Education of Young Children (NAEYC) over 20 years ago will never be fully realized for some children, Black boys especially:

> For too long we have enabled educational achievement for the very few. We have used labeling as a sorting mechanism and allowed too many children to fail. This nation can no longer afford such costly errors of exclusion. We must provide every child with the firm foundation so critical to learning in school and we must ensure that schools are prepared to meet the needs of individual children as they arrive at the school door. Only then will our nation be ready to enter the 21st Century. (NAEYC, 1995, p. 3)

This book is a loud and resounding call for change. Any attempt to enact change must come with some clear stipulations that are non-negotiable regarding injustices fueled by racism and discrimination. They must include: no more denial . . . no more excuses . . . no more tolerance . . . no more waiting . . . no more patience . . . no more. The dominant culture must be in agreement that as a nation, and certainly as a teaching force, we have an obligation (and lasting commitment) to do better by all children—including Black boys.

In the interest of achieving this monumental goal, Chapters 1 and 2 have described in great detail the historical, sociocultural, and contextual deficit view of African American boys and the negative, punitive consequences that frequently result for Black boys in early childhood education. We noted statistical data pertaining to African American boys' (1) preschool suspension and expulsion rates, (2) later academic achievement gaps, (3) overrepresentation in special education, and (4) eventual (preschool-to-prison) incarceration rates. These statistics clearly warrant the urgent need to improve and increase Black boys' access to, and participation in, high-quality culturally responsive early childhood educational experiences. As has been illustrated, it is not difficult to locate a multitude of examples in educational literature documenting the mistreatment of young Black boys, often at the hands of White female teachers.

The purpose of this chapter is to examine, discuss, and contemplate how early childhood educators can effectively create a culturally responsive learning atmosphere (classroom culture) with a strengths-based view of Black boys that values, respects, and celebrates their learning styles, culture, families, and lived experiences. It is important to caution teachers against the tendency to view learning styles as static. By this, we mean making broad claims that Black boys learn and/or are motivated to learn based on a narrow and limited repertoire (ways of knowing, interacting, etc.), which can contribute to the stereotyping of this population. We discuss this practice of essentializing in Chapter 5 in greater detail.

To accomplish this enormous yet achievable task, while avoiding the tendency to essentialize the sense-making practices, interactional styles, and experiences of Black boys, we assert that educators must first interrogate their own punitive, deficit-laden views, attitudes, and assumptions about young Black boys (particularly Black boys living in poverty) and the impact of deficit practices (whether intentional or not) on the learning and development of Black boys. Only then will teachers realize the urgency to reimagine their role as mentor/guide/facilitator with a sphere of influence to create and promote an inclusive, optimal learning atmosphere for Black boys.

CLASSROOM CULTURE:
WHAT DOES IT MEAN AND WHY DOES IT MATTER?

Culture is generally conceptualized as a system or systems of knowledge, communications, experiences, behaviors, traditions, values, beliefs, and attitudes shared and employed by any group of people. It is important to note that everyone, including those who are White, has a culture. We state this here because schools tend to engage in the practice of "othering" the culture of other people's children. We define *othering* as any action by which an individual or group becomes mentally classified in a teacher's mind as an outsider—"not one of us." This othering contributes to deficit views of non-White children in general, and Black boys in particular, as "unworthy," "a threat," and "a liability." The othering of Black boys is detrimental to their existence, because it creates an "us versus them" mentality. Challenging this mentality demands an understanding that culture is dynamic rather than static, and that becoming culturally competent is a continuous and intentional objective and process.

When children come to school with a culture that matches the dominant culture (i.e., White, middle-class culture), they possess cultural capital (e.g., education, intellect, style of speech and dress, etc.) that promotes their social mobility in a racially stratified society. Their capital accrues unearned privilege (McIntosh, 1988; Sue, Bucceri, Lin, Nadal, & Torino, 2007) and makes acquiring more capital easier and smoother. We refer to this system as a vertical view (Counsell, 2007), which further privileges one culture over another. However, we argue for the value of different cultures to be viewed from a continuum versus a vertical view. When this continuum view is achieved, the culture and identities of Black boys are recognized, valued, and respected by teachers from a cultural wealth perspective (Yosso, 2005). Cultural wealth means the "under-utilized assets Students of Color [e.g., Black boys] bring with them from their homes and communities into the classroom" (p. 70). This match or sync results in the greater probability of the often unacknowledged, unrecognized, and undervalued culture (e.g., verve) of Black boys being supported to achieve school success.

Habermas (1987) envisioned the normative consensus of beliefs and values of any social group (such as a family, school, or classroom) as the "lifeworld," expressed and interpreted by social actors (like families, teachers, and children) who strive to achieve mutual understanding through communicative action (e.g., verbal language, facial expressions, gestures, etc.). For DeVries and Zan (2012), the "entire network of interpersonal relations that make up a child's experience of a classroom" constitutes the "sociomoral atmosphere" based on constructivist theory (p. 7). Countless others in the educational literature refer to the space, place, people, materials, and activities where learning occurs as the "learning environment," "learning community," "educational setting," "learning atmosphere," "learning arrangement," "classroom climate," "learning climate," or other combination of those (Darling-Hammond & Bransford, 2005; Derman-Sparks & Edwards, 2010; Howell & Reinhard, 2015; Sullivan, 2016).

Regardless of the construct used, what is clear is that schools and classrooms function as culturalizing agents and are co-constructed and experienced by teachers and learners according to various cultural elements, traits, and factors as they pertain to the teaching and learning process. Our attempt in this book to examine and fully capture Black boys' dominant experiences in early childhood education classrooms, and the subsequent outcomes that result, is an arguably ambitious, complex, and yet necessary task. In order to contemplate recommendations that potentially can transform Black boys' experiences and dramatically improve their educational and life outcomes, we have chosen to utilize "classroom culture" as the construct with which to signify, capture, and discuss the "Black boy experience" in early childhood education—past, present, and future.

R. Wilson (n.d.) identifies three key aspects common to any formal educational experience: (1) materials and activities for children's engagement, (2) time allotted for engagement, and (3) a learning climate that either encourages or discourages active social interactions (children-to-adult interactions, and children-to-peer interactions). Wilson discussed these aspects as they pertain to supportive environments specifically (as cited in Geiken, Uhlenberg, & Yoshizawa, 2016). This chapter is dedicated to the myriad kinds of communicative actions during the teaching–learning process and the issues and concerns that result for young Black boys. Recommended materials, activities, and time considerations are discussed in greater detail in Chapters 4 and 5.

A CLASSROOM CULTURAL FRAMEWORK:
A CONTINUUM OF THREE MODELS

A study by DeVries, Haney, and Zan (1991) examined the sociomoral atmospheres in three kindergarten classrooms located in mostly Black, urban public schools for children from low-income communities. The three White kindergarten teachers largely adhered to three curricular approaches informed by different philosophical/theoretical orientations. The Direct Instruction classroom reflected behaviorist theory and practices within a "Boot Camp" sociomoral atmosphere where the teacher operated as a "drill sergeant." The constructivist classroom reflected Piaget's constructivist theory and practices within a "Community" sociomoral atmosphere and, in this case, the teacher served as a "mentor." The Eclectic classroom reflected a combined approach within a "Factory" sociomoral atmosphere in which the teacher conducted activities as a "manager."

According to DeVries et al. (2012), the sociomoral atmosphere in the Direct Instruction classroom placed an overwhelming emphasis on obedience in which the child's behavior was controlled externally by the teacher, who "tells children what to do and think" and doles out "praise for rote answers and threats or punishments for deviations in behavior" (p. 11). In stark contrast, the sociomoral atmosphere in the constructivist classroom emphasized mutual respect and cooperation, where the teacher placed great value on children's ideas, resulting in an overall positive sense of community. While the Eclectic sociomoral atmosphere was "not as negative as the Boot Camp nor as positive as the Community," the teacher nonetheless pressured children into obedience toward the "production of academic work" (p. 17).

If the foundation for social identity and related competencies relies heavily on context and relationships, then we certainly can make the argument that different philosophical/theoretical orientations and beliefs about teaching and learning result in different classroom cultures that have the potential to encourage, or diametrically repress, various competencies in Black boys. As a result, all interactions between and among children and educators impact children's social and moral experience and development in both helpful and hurtful ways, as described in Chapter 2.

As described by DeVries and Zan (2012), "interpersonal relations are the dynamic context in which children construct their ideas and feelings about themselves, the world of people, and the world of objects" (p. 40). If educators want Black boys to construct a positive, strengths-based, empowered self-identity in which they feel and view themselves as capable, intellectual, talented, creative, and adventurous (just to name a few attributes), then that would suggest that educators must create and cultivate classroom cultures that help promote and support those outcomes.

When it comes to Black boys, the research overwhelmingly demonstrates that their early childhood educational experiences tend to be dominated by either a Boot Camp or Factory classroom culture, with clear consequences for learning and developmental outcomes. Early childhood educators who operate as either drill sergeants or managers, with teacher-directed instruction and a disciplinary approach that demands obedience and compliance, also impact the interrelationships that develop and the resultant teacher expectations.

The Need for Healthy, Unbiased Attachment

Social interactions between the classroom teacher and individual children contribute directly to the teacher's ability to develop a rapport and meaningful relationship with each child. Attachment theory, according to Bowlby (1988), explains how caregivers' different kinds of responses and interactions with young children impact children's learning and development, in either positive or negative ways.

Through daily, ongoing exchanges between the teacher and individual children, Black boys quickly come to understand whether their social surroundings are "safe or unsafe, loving or hostile, coercive or cooperative, satisfying or unsatisfying" (DeVries & Zan, 2012, p. 40). Ongoing experiences in their social surroundings serve to guide and inform young children's construction of "internal working models" that become the social lens through which they view and interpret their world and the people in it (Bowlby, 1982, p. 354).

If educators want to maximize young Black boys' learning and development, then they must strive to develop healthy bonds and secure attachments with Black boys. This strengths-based view depends heavily on suspending deficit thinking that takes the position that Black boys and their "families are at fault for poor academic performance because: (a) students enter school without the normative cultural knowledge and skills; and (b) parents neither value nor support their child's education" (Yosso, 2005, p. 75). Only then can key caregivers and educators successfully empower Black boys to construct healthy self-identities as capable learners. Black boys know that their voices are heard, valued, and understood, and they are further empowered with agency to seek and fulfill their wants and needs when significant adults have developed strong bonds with them. However, what happens when child-care providers and early childhood educators view young Black boys and their families, particularly those who reside in low-income or high-poverty communities, through a deficit-laden lens informed by racist ideology? Can deficit-laden views compromise the development of healthy bonds and secure attachments with Black boys?

Prior to 1950, general perceptions of children living in poverty in the United States were guided and informed largely by eugenics beliefs about intelligence, talent, and heredity along the lines of race and social class (Counsell & Agran, 2013; Counsell & Boody, 2013). Historically, the "culture of poverty" described by Lewis (1959), as cited in Fischer (1985), was generally viewed as a "lower-class value system that denigrates hard work, discipline, and ambition and sacrifices future reward for immediate gratification" (p. 247) and included an overrepresentation of African Americans. Accordingly, the unavoidable outcome, "poverty resulting from slothfulness" (Fischer, 1985, p. 247), was presumed and used to further justify racial stereotypes, deficit assumptions, and limited life outcomes (as cited in Counsell & Boody, 2013).

This racist and deficit-laden eugenics view of people residing in poverty continued to underlie investigations examining the role that environment plays in intellectual development, which led some to believe in notions of "cultural deprivation" in the 1960s and 1970s (Counsell & Boody, 2013). Despite evidence that long ago rejected cultural deprivation as biased marginalization of non-White groups by some in the dominant culture, assumptions about racial and ethnic groups who reside in low-income neighborhoods continue to persist and influence adult–child interactions and relationships (Brantlinger, 2003). Cultural deprivation assumptions include beliefs about whether families read to their children, visit the local library, have a home library, or play board games. Is it possible that racist ideology, like cultural deprivation assumptions, negatively impact the quality of bonds and attachments formed between teachers and Black boys? What is the likelihood that insecure bonds and unhealthy attachments simultaneously lower teachers' expectations for Black boys?

The Need for Unbiased, High Teacher Expectations

Teachers who uncritically equate high-income status (and particular racial groups like White children) with advanced achievement and high intelligence are operating according to unexamined White privilege. Teachers who uncritically presume that living in poverty (particularly for racial groups like some Black boys) equates with low skills and behavior problems operate according to racialized assumptions grounded in racist ideology. Children who are presumed to be more capable with higher aptitudes are granted access to higher-track educational opportunities (e.g., enrichment activities, gifted-and-talented placement, honors classes, etc.) that generally lead to higher academic outcomes (White privilege). In stark contrast, children who are presumed to be less capable counterparts (particularly Black boys) based on racist ideological assumptions and beliefs are granted access to lower-track educational opportunities (e.g., remedial instruction, special education, vocational training) that generally lead to lower academic outcomes.

This utilitarian meritocratic worldview of learners has been used widely in public education to rank and sort children, most often based on standardized test scores (Counsell, 2007). Test scores are then used to warrant dissemination of correlated educational opportunities based on merit (or lack of merit) in a tracking process that is declared to be a "fair and neutral means of providing access to economic rewards" (Oakes, 1993, p. 90).

Within the confines of classroom settings, we easily can observe what happens when teachers view children with a deficit-laden view versus a strengths-based view and how teachers' assumptions impact learning outcomes. As indicated earlier, when teachers make biased, racist assumptions about groups of children like African American boys, a correlation results between high or low expectations and high or low academic performance outcomes. Referred to as the Pygmalion phenomenon, this seminal research completed by Rosenthal and Jacobson (1968) revealed the interrelationship between teachers' expectations and learners' self-fulfilling prophecies.

According to the Pygmalion phenomenon, when teachers expect students to do well and show intellectual growth, the students' growth reflects those expectations. When teachers do not have such expectations, performance and growth are not encouraged and may even be discouraged (Counsell & Boody, 2013). Hence, teachers' expectations are paramount and non-negotiable in maximizing young children's learning and development, especially for Black boys. Almost 50 years later, research has continued to demonstrate that low expectations persist for Black boys in low-income schools (Ford, 2013; Hallinger, Bickman, & Davis, 1996; Kennedy, 1995; McKown & Weinstein, 2008).

THE INTERSECTION OF ATTACHMENT
AND EXPECTATIONS WITH EPIGENETICS

Teachers clearly play a lead role in how they choose to control and influence the kind of classroom culture they develop, promote, and maintain to support young children's learning and development. On the other hand, teachers do not have any control over each individual learner's innate temperament, interests, talents, skills, aptitudes, and abilities. Increasingly, current research reveals the complex interaction between the child's genes and environment (including the home culture and classroom culture) in ways that influence traits and characteristics.

According to probabilistic epigenesis, specific traits, characteristics, or behaviors may or may not emerge over the course of development depending on whether specific environmental conditions (life experiences) activate the child's existing genetic potential (Gottlieb, 1997, 2003). This means that every child has many more possible developmental pathways than are ever realized.

It is the child's environment that overtly influences and controls which parts of the child's genome are activated. Hence, the classroom culture experienced by young Black boys in particular can significantly enhance or impede which genes will be expressed. Since any individual child's genome is an unknown mystery, it is important to maximize young Black boys' access and exposure to a full range of educational opportunities, enrichment, and experiences in order to optimize the likelihood that their hidden gifts, talents, abilities, and skills will emerge (Ford, 2013).

Teachers working with Black boys must ask themselves honestly and candidly: What is happening (and not happening) in preschool classrooms nationwide that would cause African American children to be suspended out of school at a rate that is 3.6 times higher than for other groups? Why are 45% of all preschool suspensions African American children, yet African American children are only 19% of the preschool enrollment? According to Gilliam (2005), 91% of the African American preschoolers who were expelled were Black boys. What does this say about Black boys' experiences in preschool classrooms today? Who are the preschool teachers who are suspending Black boys at alarming, overrepresented rates?

Data are compelling regarding the demographics of teachers suspending Black boys at alarming, overrepresented rates. According to one study of 64 White college students' perceptions of randomized faces conducted at the University of Iowa, participants frequently associated guns at faster rates after seeing Black children's faces in comparison to White children's faces. These data beg the question, are these results an anomaly or representative of the attitudes and beliefs of the larger White society, including White female teachers? It is essential, critical, and culturally responsive to reflect upon how these kinds of racist views of Black boys play out in preschool classrooms. We must consider why the criminalization of Black boys, beginning in early childhood education (as discussed in Chapter 2), originates early on in the "cultural deprivation" mindset of those entrusted with the education and care of Black boys. We must consider the myriad ways this criminalization ultimately ascribes to African American families and communities lack of moral character and virtues (such as honesty, trustworthiness, hard work, loyalty, and ethics) and consequently how every Black boy is looked upon by the dominant culture with suspicion.

If preschool teachers are uncritical practitioners who do not reflect on their own lifeworld view (attitudes, assumptions, and beliefs) concerning Black boys, they are likely to be equally unreflective and uncritical about the deficit-laden practices and deficit outcomes that result. Rather than examine and interrogate how these practices potentially advance or hinder young Black boys' learning and development, uncritical, unreflective, and culturally unresponsive teachers place the onus for learning and developmental outcomes largely on Black boys (children), families, and communities. Given that academic gaps and disparities persist, the blame must not be assigned largely to the child, family, and neighborhood. Uncritical, unreflective, and culturally unresponsive teachers like this may even resort to polemic notions of "cultural deprivation" (as described earlier) as further validation for blaming families and communities, which alleviates some of their responsibility as educators. Blaming the "victim" is counterproductive.

It is crucial to consider how early childhood educators can develop a healthy bond and secure attachment to young Black boys when they perceive them through a deficit-laden lens. How can Black boys develop a healthy self-identity with confident voice and agency in the absence of a strong bond and secure attachment to caregivers—specifically early childhood educators—that reassures them that they are safe, nurtured, valued, affirmed, and loved?

If early childhood educators harbor a deficit-oriented view of Black boys that goes unchallenged and unchecked, deficit-laden practices invariably result. For example, deficit-laden tracking minimizes or eliminates access to enrichment, higher-order thinking, and challenging learning opportunities and experiences. It is then no surprise that minimized learning and developmental outcomes are the end product of deficit-laden practices. Limiting educational opportunities and learning experiences serves to potentially suppress the expression of individual Black boys' gifts, talents, skills, and abilities, which, without urgent intervention, may permanently fade over time. Ford (2010) speaks extensively about gifted Black boys who underachieve for such reasons.

This tragic educational reality, referred to as a "cycle of deficit" (Counsell, 2017a), results in the direst consequences for historically marginalized groups like Black boys (see Figure 3.1). In this cycle, uncritical, unreflective, and culturally unresponsive teachers believe that deficits exist, informed by their unexamined, unchallenged, biased, and most often racist deficit-laden view of Black boys. Based on a deficit belief, the teacher then sees or, more accurately, perceives deficits in the learning and development of Black boys. The teacher's perceived deficits, in turn, lower the teacher's learning and developmental expectations for this group of boys. The teacher's lowered expectations are then used to select and provide educational opportunities that are aligned with the teacher's deficit expectations, and hence less challenging, while simultaneously limiting Black boys' access to rigorous, culturally relevant enrichment experiences. The decision to provide opportunities based on (mis)perceived deficits leads to lowered learning and developmental outcomes that discount and do not reflect the child's learning aptitude, prior knowledge and experiences, and potential. In the end, the child's lowered learning and developmental outcomes verify the teacher's original belief that deficits existed, and the deficit results are further confirmation, thereby completing the "cycle of deficit."

Lowered teacher expectations lead to lower and negative learning and developmental opportunities and outcomes. While we have referenced how

Figure 3.1. Cycle of Deficit

Source: Counsell (2017a).

White female teachers tend to be the majority contributors to the deficit scenarios experienced by Black boys in early childhood education, this does not mean that other racial groups of teachers, male or female, are automatically immune or that color inherently equals consciousness, because that is sadly not always the case. Nevertheless, the frequency with which non-White children, and Black boys in particular, will encounter a White female teacher who is not culturally competent is far greater given that the demographic background of teachers is 84% White and 16% non-White (McFarland et al., 2017). According to their report, this trend has shown little change over the decade, since the majority of students enrolled in teacher education programs, especially early childhood education, continues to be White, female, and middle class.

TEACHER CANDIDATES AND TEACHERS DISCOUNTING DATA: A CASE IN POINT

In a methods course where students are exposed to the intersection of social–emotional development and social studies, they were reading and discussing the *2013–2014 Civil Rights Data Collection: A First Look* (U.S.

Department of Education Office for Civil Rights, 2016), specifically the section devoted to "school discipline" (discussed throughout this book). It was pointed out to the students that these data are based on the following:

a. Districts—16,758 school districts; 95,507 schools; 50,035,744 students
b. Gender—51.4% boys and 48.6% girls
c. Race/Ethnicity—racial demographics that comprise 50.3% White, 24.7% Hispanic or Latino of any race, 15.5% Black or African American, 4.8% Asian, 3.1% two or more races, 1.1% American Indian or Alaska Native, and 0.4% Native Hawaiian or other Pacific Islander

Many students enrolled in the course (White, Black, and Latinx) found the suspension and expulsion rates of Black children, boys especially, as early as preschool troubling, and yet they still, individually and collectively, looked for contradictions and discrepancies; they blamed families and, in some cases, the children for these high rates of suspension and expulsion. In fact, many defaulted to the unexamined beliefs that the lack of family involvement in the child's education was to blame, and in some instances they blamed these high rates of suspension and expulsion on the child's lack of school readiness and unwillingness to follow classroom rules. Thus, they looked to the families and children in justifying these national data, thereby absolving themselves and schools of any responsibility.

Unsure whether the teacher candidates fully understood the significance of these national data, the instructor asked whether they thought factors other than assigning blame to children and families, such as teacher attitudes, teacher expectations, implicit bias, racism, and/or discrimination, were important considerations. When asked to consider these factors, teacher candidates began to share examples from the schools where they were completing their student teaching. For example, one student shared that she frequently noticed Black boys in her school waiting outside the principal's office. Other students, including some teacher candidates of color, echoed this same observation to explain and justify the reasons for the high rates of suspension and expulsion reported in the Office for Civil Rights data. The overwhelming response was that race was irrelevant and inconsequential to these national data, evidencing a colorblind analysis.

In another example, these same data were shared in a talk to teachers at a professional organization for early childhood teachers. Many of these veteran teachers, in common with the teacher candidates above, made implicit and explicit references to race, ethnicity, culture, and/or socioeconomic status of children and their families to justify and explain reasons for the behavior of Black children, boys especially. For example, one teacher's comments were grounded in social and academic stereotypes of African

Americans and families living in poverty. Still others pointed to "dysfunctional" families (e.g., single-parent homes, exposure to crime and violence) to explain these national data. Strikingly, across both teacher candidates and teachers, few thought race(ism) or discrimination played any part in the high rates of suspension and expulsion.

BOOT CAMPS AND FACTORIES DOMINATE BLACK BOYS' EXPERIENCES

Based on the two scenarios described above, involving the teacher candidates and the veteran teachers, it is not surprising that the classroom experiences of Black children, Black boys especially, continue to reflect Boot Camp (militaristic practices) and Factory classroom cultures that undermine their social–emotional development, not to mention limiting their promise, potential, and possibility. The reality is that Black boys who have the greatest need for well-prepared, thoughtful, critical, culturally competent early childhood educators who can deliver a high-quality early childhood education experience (see Chapter 2) are also the least likely to receive high-quality early care and education experiences (Barnett, Hustedt, Friedman, Stevenson Boyd, & Ainsworth, 2007). Without access to high-quality preschool, African American and Latino children, and children from low-income families, are far less likely to be prepared to start kindergarten than their peers (Johns, 2016).

Research suggests that teachers who utilize a Direct Instruction curriculum generally embrace a behaviorist philosophical approach to teaching and learning that emphasizes a classroom culture of discipline much like the Boot Camp or Factory classroom cultures. For example, one study by Stipek (2004) examined the nature of instruction utilized in 314 kindergarten and 1st-grade classrooms from 155 schools in 48 school districts across three states serving largely children of color living in poverty. Among the 314 classrooms, the majority of teachers (92%) were female and approximately 4.5% were male (another 3.5% did not respond to the gender question). The vast majority of teachers, 73%, were White, with just 7% identified as African American, 5% Hispanic, 4% Asian, and 3% "other" or "mixed" ethnicity; 8% did not identify their race/ethnicity.

Stipek's (2004) study revealed that the socioeconomic status and racial school demographics corresponded directly with a specific type of social climate, theoretical approach, and teaching practices (classroom culture). According to teacher ratings, Stipek determined that didactic, direct instructional teaching with an isolated basic skills emphasis and negative social climates (like Boot Camps and Factories) dominated the teaching–learning experience at the low-income and high-poverty schools.

Three specific reasons emerged to explain the possible justification for selected teaching methods and practices. First, teachers argued that children living in poverty who struggle academically must "master the 'basics' before they can benefit from problem-solving, critical thinking, or more inquiry-oriented, constructivist practices" (Stipek, 2004, p. 552). Hence, perceived "deficits" result in lowered expectations and subsequent limitations placed on learning opportunities, which further minimize potential outcomes and the likelihood that gifts, talents, and abilities of Black boys will be recognized, validated, and allowed to be expressed in the early childhood classroom.

Second, teachers referred to preferences on the part of families in economically challenged communities, particularly African American parents, for basic skills and didactic teaching. Previous studies suggest that African American families are more authoritative and directive in their own parenting and teaching interactions (Hart, Burts, & Charlesworth, 1997; Lubeck, 1994; Powell, 1994; Stipek & Byler, 1997). For this reason, Delpit (1995) proposed that African American families living in poverty may be more comfortable with highly structured learning. It is also possible that African American families, as learners themselves, are products of this teaching approach. Thus, constructivist theory and practices are unfamiliar, and parents may pressure teachers to adhere to the more familiar didactic, direct, skills-based approach.

The problem with the characterization of Black families as more authoritative and directive is that the methods used to substantiate such a myopic view do not account for the unrelenting challenge involved in forging a mother-to-son or father-to-son relationship in a context where African American boys are largely presumed to be "bad" or "troublemakers." This deficit view contributes in many ways to the persistent inequality regarding educational attainment and academic achievement for African American boys. For this reason, we argue that when consideration is given to the hostile context of raising Black boys, not only is it necessary that Black families exercise a higher degree of control, but they must do so with a higher degree of warmth to offset the differential treatment of their sons, both in and outside of schools.

Third, teachers serving both children living in poverty and children of color are generally less experienced and less well trained in using constructivist theory and practices; hence, they find it easier to implement commercialized, packaged, scripted material. It is equally important to note that teachers in the 2004 Stipek study rated African American children, particularly boys, as more aggressive than White or Hispanic children. In response to this perception, teachers imposed "stricter control" with more structured, teacher-dominated instruction in order to manage and "maintain order" in their classrooms. This hyper-focus on discipline and controlling Black boys is, sadly, no different from how they are treated in society.

As highlighted in Chapters 1 and 2, the trend toward excessive discipline for African American children in general, and Black boys in particular, is a relentless running narrative. Emdin (2016) has described classroom cultures that Black boys most often experience as "oppressive places" focused on rules and discipline, in which teachers employ "a tough hand to keep them in line" (p. 5).

Creating Classroom Cultures That Value, Respect, and Celebrate Black Boys

As elaborated extensively throughout this book, Cabrera (2013) was on the mark when she pointedly declared that "we know more about why minority children fail than we know about why they succeed" (p. 4). In the case of Black boys, previous chapters and discussions have amply documented the legacy of misguided missteps, mistakes, misperceptions, misunderstandings, and misinterpretations of Black boys as learners and the subsequent deficit-laden choices and outcomes that have resulted.

It is imperative that culturally competent, critical, and reflective practitioners use the negative examples of what teachers *should not do* to instead inform what they *should do* according to research and evidence-based practices and the basic humanity of other people's children—in the case of this book, Black boys. From this point forward, we embrace a mindful, dramatic paradigm shift away from the longstanding narrative of deficits about Black boys in favor of a transformed narrative focused on Black boys' assets and strengths within a constructivist, democratic classroom culture of empowerment.

Constructivist, Culturally Responsive Democratic Culture of Empowerment

Like all young children, Black boys are intrinsically curious about the world, with a desire to figure out how the world works (Piaget, 1973, 1981). Many children, and Black boys are no exception, enjoy self-directed and physically active learning in social groups with their peers (Boykin & Noguera, 2011; Noguera, 2008). Since constructivist theory encourages children to construct knowledge as they openly engage in their surroundings, actively interpreting their experiences in academic, physical, and social worlds (DeVries & Kohlberg, 1987; DeVries & Zan, 2012), this approach to classroom culture is a promising match to Black boys' learning style.

For Piaget (1981), a child's intelligence continually develops and emerges as the child organizes and makes sense of the surrounding world, including everyone, everything, and all life experiences encountered. This view or interpretation is likewise compatible with current brain research and the important role that environment plays in epigenetics. Cognitive schemes are internally formed as children act on objects in the world.

Design aspects of learning activities and projects in constructivist classrooms are highly engaging and intrinsically motivating to children as they identify their own compelling questions and figure out how to make something happen to achieve an intended goal or outcome (Brooks, 2011; Kamii & DeVries, 1993). Young children learn to apply academic content, concepts, and relationships in practical ways that are meaningful to them within projects that involve design processes (Hmelo, Holton, & Kolodner, 2000; Schunn, 2009).

For young children in particular, interests fuel their mental construction of relationships as they interact with their surroundings (Piaget, 1981). Children of all ages, races, and abilities are more likely to exert their fullest attention and mental energy toward investigating and finding solutions to problems or achieving goals and outcomes that matter most to them (Counsell, Uhlenberg, & Zan, 2013). Black boys are no exception.

All young children benefit and prosper from multiple and varied opportunities to actively observe, engage in, interact with, and interpret authentic, open-ended learning experiences with hands-on multisensory materials and rich opportunities for group work within diverse, inclusive settings (Counsell, Peat, et al., 2015; Counsell & Wright, 2016). This approach is particularly advantageous to Black boys in particular because of the concept of verve (discussed above and later in this chapter), which is defined as the receptiveness on the part of Black boys to enjoy relatively high levels of sensate stimulation. Further, we argue that all young children enjoy hands-on experiences, working with manipulative materials, and multiple stimuli (Boykin & Noguera, 2011; Murphy & Nesby, 2002; Watkins, 2002).

CONSTRUCTIVIST TEACHERS: EMPATHETIC COMMUNITY MENTORS

Constructivist mentors are professionally prepared to value children's prior knowledge and experience, including cultural traditions, routines, customs, and core beliefs that help personalize learning in culturally responsive ways (Sampson & Garrison-Wade, 2011; Waddell, 2010). Connecting children's learning to prior knowledge and experiences is a mutually respectful constructivist and culturally responsive practice that makes learning meaningful and relevant, and simultaneously motivates and elicits children's active learning engagement (Crumpton & Gregory, 2011; Shields, 1995).

Constructivist mentors guide and facilitate children's construction of mental relationships by (1) engaging children's interest, (2) inspiring active exploration and investigation, and (3) fostering cooperation between adults and children/students and among peers (DeVries & Zan, 2012). The ongoing experiences and interactions between adults and children within their social surroundings, as noted earlier, serve as the social lens through which children view and interpret their world and the people in it. Constructivist mentors nurture and promote inclusive learning communities that embrace and celebrate children's cultural similarities and differences.

The advantages, encompassing learning and developmental benefits, among other things, of placing Black boys in constructivist classroom settings are clear and numerous. A constructivist curriculum and approach must guarantee that all constructivist teachers, especially those who are White females, are prepared to mentor Black boys in culturally responsive ways. Constructivist mentors must embrace a strengths-based view of Black boys wherein they hold high expectations in order to maximize learning opportunities and outcomes. While it cannot be assumed that teachers (novice or veteran) easily and/or quickly can translate knowledge into culturally relevant pedagogy, all teachers must become aware of the many cultures they are a part of and how these cultural differences might affect their teaching and their students' learning.

As noted at the outset of this chapter, the social network of interpersonal relations is at the heart of every classroom culture, whether it is a Boot Camp, Factory, or Community culture. Within that network of interactions, empathetic mentors who teach Black boys in constructivist communities must be mindful of and fully utilize culturally responsive interactions that "cater to the social and cultural needs, norms, realities, experiences, and preferences" (Warren, 2013, p. 176) of Black boys, such as Boykin's Afrocentric cultural characteristics.

Constructivist mentors can effectively apply Cole and Boykin's (2008) Afrocentric cultural characteristics to (1) guide and inform teaching practices; (2) structure learning activities and experiences; (3) select materials; and (4) develop and sustain a learning community that encourages full participation (see Figure 3.2).

For example, from an Afrocentric perspective, culturally competent and responsive teachers use Black boys' social, affective, psychological, physical, academic, and cognitive characteristics and skills to develop effective ways to converse and engage with young Black boys that are both mindful and intentional. Similarly, a culturally competent and responsive mentor would structure and design learning activities that appeal to Black boys' Afrocentric cultural preferences. Such activities would fully utilize Black boys' physical movement and active engagement, with multiple opportunities to use hands-on learning and manipulatives.

At the center of culturally responsive interactions is empathetic teaching (T. C. Howard, 2010; Milner, 2010) and the humanity of all children, and Black boys in particular. According to Warren (2013), teachers (particularly White female teachers) who utilize empathy when teaching learners across differences are better prepared to negotiate interactions in ways that result in more positive academic and behavioral student

Figure 3.2. Boykin's Afrocentric Cultural Characteristics

Cultural Characteristic	Description
Spirituality	Belief in a nonmaterial force that influences all of life; religious; faithful; optimistic; resilient.
Harmony	Keen observation skill as demonstrated by (1) ability to read the environment well, and (2) ability to read people well (reads nonverbal cues and body language well). Quickly notices injustices and discrepancies in what is said and done, as well as how students are treated.
Affective	Sensitive and emotional; easily excited; impulsive—may react before thinking. Easily angered; loves and hates strongly.
Movement	Enjoys being mobile and active; tactile and kinesthetic learner; dislikes being sedentary; prefers to be physically and mentally engaged.
Verve	High levels of energy; easily excited; physically active when engaged and mentally stimulated; can become "loud" when excited or engaged.
Communalism	A strong need to belong; strong need for affiliation; group oriented; social and interdependent; extroverted and people oriented. Wants to be liked, appreciated, and respected by others. Sense of family and community is strong.
Expressive Individualism	Creative; risk taker; dares to be different; dramatic; clever; original. Likes to play with ideas, words, language, dressing, and to embellish what appears commonplace or bland.
Oral Tradition	Prefers to communicate orally; blunt with comments and feedback; direct with words and feedback or comments; likes playing with words (jokes, puns, riddles, proverbs, analogies, etc.).
Social Time Perspective	Polychronic; time is not seen as a limited commodity—there is unlimited time; time is social; time should be enjoyed; can do more than one thing at a time; many have difficulty with managing time and organization; pleasure and work go hand-in-hand.

outcomes. An empathetic concern, as characterized by M. H. Davis (1994) and Eisenberg and Strayer (1997), is "an emotional connection or 'feeling with' an individual that creates a heightened awareness of that individual's plight" (Warren, 2013, p. 177).

When thinking about developing culturally responsive constructivist mentors, it is imperative to highlight the clear distinction between encouraging "heightened awareness" with understanding of individual learners' circumstances and operating according to "deficit assumptions." Educators must understand the unique (i.e., gendered, racialized, contextualized, and context-specific) needs and circumstances of Black boys and families without enacting racial stereotypes and assumptions. Just as constructivist mentors closely observe and listen to children's ideas and perspectives during explorations and investigations, they also must pay attention to and strive to understand Black boys' academic, cognitive, social, and cultural perspectives, and use such vital contextualized information to guide and inform the teaching–learning process.

As Warren (2013) reminded us, Whiteness itself "represents a layer of social and cultural perspective most akin to White racial norms, truths, expectations, and experiences" (p. 179). For these reasons, constructivist mentors who strive to be culturally responsive must always be critical and reflective about their teaching, practices, and interactions with Black boys. As Warren (2013) concluded, teachers (White or non-White) who demonstrate empathy in their ongoing interactions with learners of color are more likely to build strong, trusting relationships with learners and families; develop positive classroom cultures; be more willing to take risks; be more flexible; and take more proactive initiatives to ensure favorable learner outcomes.

The constructivist and culturally responsive mentor designs the learning environment to encourage and ensure that all students have equitable access to child-centered, child-directed exploration and investigation of materials available in developmental centers (e.g., blocks, dramatic play, cooking, language/literacy, science, and art). As valued community members, children in constructivist, democratic learning communities can explore and investigate materials and activities independently, with a partner, in small groups, or in large-group arrangements. Working together capitalizes on Black children's strengths of cultural, social, and cognitive skills that enable them to sustain play interactions among classmates. Collaboration requires children to cooperate. As children cooperate with adults and classmates during explorations and investigations, they utilize higher-order critical thinking skills when:

a.   communicating their points of view (perspective taking)
b.   sharing materials
c.   communicating ideas
d.   asking questions
e.   negotiating project goals and agendas
f.   brainstorming and being creative
g.   problem solving

An accessible curriculum is one in which all aspects of the curriculum (e.g., environment, goals, content, instructional methods and interactions, assessments, books, toys, and materials) invite active participation of all children, regardless of disability or special needs (Counsell, 2009; Counsell

& Sander, 2016; Counsell & Wright, 2016; Palincsar, Magnusson, Collins, & Cutter, 2001; Williams & Veomett, 2007). Black boys (not all) and other children, who struggle academically, benefit greatly from active engagement rather than teacher-directed instruction (Bodovski & Farkas, 2007) as well as from instruction that is culturally responsive.

Democratic Community Membership

Constructivist learning communities operate democratically as all community members (adults and children) are respected, and all ideas, perspectives, and experiences are shared and mutually valued. Establishing mutually respectful, collaborative relationships communicates to Black boys that adults care about them as individuals, have high expectations for them as learners, and actively support their ongoing construction of knowledge and understanding that are likewise advocated by asset- or strengths-based research (Graves & Howes, 2011; Hughes, 2011). Democratic membership empowers children to (1) have a voice in what happens; (2) help shape the course of study; (3) help decide when, where, why, how, and with whom learning takes place; and (4) understand how progress will be assessed (Kohn, 1999, 2006). Listening to what Black boys have to say, and acknowledging their prior knowledge, interests, agendas, and ideas, communicates to them that what they think and feel matters to teachers. When teachers work together with children in general, and Black boys in particular, to mutually define how they want to operate, act, think, and learn as a community, teachers become fellow travelers as they co-construct meanings and relationships in a shared journey of learning, growth, and empowerment (Counsell & Boody, 2013; Wright, Counsell, & Tate, 2015).

In addition to the learning and opportunity gaps frequently cited and discussed in educational research, as the National Education Association (2011) identified, there are three additional gaps that are equally relevant— attitude, relationship, and relevance gaps. Socializing Black boys with active empowerment within constructivist, democratic classroom cultures addresses head-on the "attitude gap" of learned helplessness, low self-esteem, and lack of racial and gender pride, which is attributed largely to teachers' low expectations.

Preparing early childhood educators as culturally responsive constructivist mentors who value, respect, and appreciate Black boys promotes the strong rapport and secure attachment needed to eliminate the "relationship gap" experienced by Black boys who are subjected to uncritical, unreflective, non–culturally responsive teachers who perceive only deficits. Finally, encouraging children to pursue compelling questions and problems that matter to them is the counter-response to the "relevance gap" experienced by Black boys during isolated basic skill-drill lessons that lack real-life meaning.

Culturally responsive constructivist early childhood educators who teach Black boys will replace the cycle of deficit with a transformed "cycle of strength" (see Figure 3.3). In this cycle, critical, reflective, and culturally responsive practitioners believe that strengths and potential exist in Black boys—a belief that is informed by their awareness of racial and cultural learning styles. Founded on a strengths-based belief, teachers see and perceive strengths in children's learning and development. The teachers' perceived strengths, in turn, raise their learning and developmental expectations for Black boys. Teachers' higher or more rigorous expectations are then used to select and provide Black boys with more challenging and culturally relevant lessons and activities, which encourage higher-order thinking skills. The decision to provide opportunities based on children's strengths leads to elevated learning and developmental outcomes that largely reflect children's learning opportunities and experiences. In the end, Black boys' higher learning and developmental outcomes "verify" teachers' original belief and high expectations that strengths existed. Given the aforementioned, we now turn to classroom meetings to promote a sense of community.

Figure 3.3. Cycle of Strength

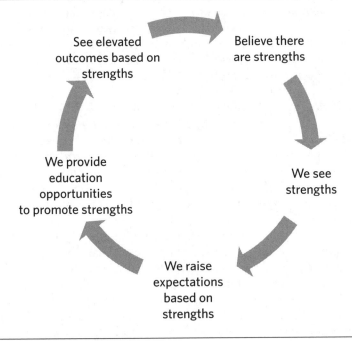

Source: Counsell (2017a).

Classroom Community Meetings: More on Being Culturally Responsive

The class community meeting is a group time held at either the beginning or end of the school day to discuss any issues or concerns related to specific class activities, community member interactions, or community rules, policies, or procedures. Generally speaking, class meetings provide children the opportunity to exchange ideas in a respectful, caring atmosphere. Just as all community members are granted full access to cooperative learning groups, projects, and collaborative explorations and investigations, so are all community members guaranteed voice and agency to fully participate in the problem-solving and decisionmaking process. Guided by teachers, class meetings empower children to help identify issues, reflect on their options and choices made, and consider the subsequent outcomes in order to make better choices that value and respect everyone (Developmental Studies Center, 1996; Vance, 2015). In addition to providing Black boys with opportunities to think about, discuss, and challenge how they want to be as a class community member, meetings cover other topics that relate to interpersonal issues like rule making, decisionmaking, and problem solving.

Chapter 2 described a scenario in which Joshua was harshly reprimanded by the student teacher when he stepped out of line, whereas the White boys, who also stepped out of line momentarily, were gently nudged back into place. As discussed throughout this chapter, this student teacher was uncritical about her dramatically differential treatment of Joshua in contrast to the White boys. The 3rd-grade teacher's deficit-laden view of Joshua as a low-performing student who previously attended a low-performing school largely informed the student teacher's deficit view of Joshua. A White female classmate also observed the differential treatment and took up Joshua's mistreatment and verbally reprimanded him as well.

This type of mistreatment of Black boys by majority White female teachers would not happen if they strived to be critical, reflective, and culturally competent practitioners who taught with empathy and cultivated a constructivist classroom culture using culturally responsive practices to build caring relationships that empowered children with voice and agency. If this was a constructivist democratic community, the mentor or the children could announce at a class meeting that as a community they needed to revisit the rules and procedures they agreed upon with regard to walking as a class in the hallways. This would allow the children to re-examine the rules with adults as fellow travelers and co-construct together whether any changes or revisions were needed.

It is equally important to invite and welcome Black families to visit the classroom to collaborate, observe, and participate in learning activities, projects, and investigations. The need to allow Black families the opportunity to share their viewpoints and perspectives on a regular basis cannot be overstated or overestimated. This will help communicate to Black parents that their voice, perceptions, experiences, and insights are valued and appreciated as extended members of the community and as decisionmakers in their Black sons' educational journeys.

CONCLUSION

As stated at the outset of this chapter, the purpose was to examine, discuss, challenge, and contemplate how early childhood educators can effectively create education with a culturally responsive strengths-based view of Black boys that celebrates, values, respects, and validates their creative sense-making, intellectual resources, and culture. This chapter challenges educators to interrogate their practices, worldviews, attitudes, and assumptions about Black boys. Then, educators can begin to contemplate the potential impact (intentional or not) chosen practices have on young Black boys' learning and development.

Three types of classroom cultures (Boot Camp, Factory, and Community) were considered and discussed. The key role that classroom teachers play in establishing classroom cultures, particularly for Black boys, was examined in relation to forming secure attachments, setting high and positive expectations, and how attachments and expectations contribute to maximizing epigenetics. A review and analysis of research examining Black boys' early childhood experience reveal that Black boys are overwhelmingly subjected to Boot Camp or Factory classroom cultures that historically have helped maintain the achievement and opportunity gaps and have perpetuated the egregious preschool-to-prison pipeline.

Increasingly research demonstrates the potential advantages and benefits of providing Black boys with early childhood experiences in a constructivist, democratic, and culturally responsive classroom community using cultural practices to optimize and honor Black boys' learning opportunities and outcomes. As noted, it is imperative to prepare constructivist educators as critical, reflective, and culturally competent practitioners with the essential empathy needed to develop awareness and understanding of individual learners—like Black boys—across differences, without racist ideology and assumptions.

In brief, creating a democratic, culturally responsive community classroom culture where Black boys can succeed—where their light can shine—can finally fulfill NAEYC's (1995) visionary call to better prepare schools to meet the needs of children and thus cultural groups upon arrival at school. Chapter 4 further investigates how to promote and support Black boys' development of a healthy identity, voice, and agency, with specific recommendations using African American children's literature. In Chapter 5, specific materials, activities, and time considerations are discussed to promote and support Black boys' learning and development within constructivist, culturally responsive, democratic classroom cultures.

CHAPTER 4

Developing Self-Identity and Agency in Black Boys

"Why Ryheim Does Not Like to Read"

Ryheim, an African American boy, is a rambunctious, imaginative, and intelligent 2nd-grader who asks a lot of questions and always has an elaborate story full of intimate, layered details to share during class meetings. Ryheim's classmates, almost all of whom are White, are captivated by his way with words and always ask him to tell a story. He is a good reader but he does not like to read. When his White female teacher (Ms. Woods) invites the class to select a book from the classroom library, Ryheim is always the last to choose a book. When he finally selects a book, he retreats to a corner of the classroom, away from the other children and teacher. As usual, his teacher walks around to talk with groups of children about their chosen books. She typically asks them to map out their story (i.e., the setting [Where? When?], character [Who?], problem [What is the main problem?], and solution [How is the problem solved?]). Hiding from his teacher, Ryheim is caught daydreaming and talking to his classmates about a trip to the zoo with his dad. When asked by Ms. Woods to tell her about his book, Ryheim, with a sad look and much frustration, asks, "How come there ain't no Black boys in these books?"

Too often Black children, especially Black boys, quickly lose interest in reading. Many complain of finding little relevance in books. This hinders their identity and sense of self as learners. Approximately a quarter of the total children's books published in 2015 were picture books, and about half of those depicted nonhuman characters (e.g., animals, trucks, etc.). While those that remained did not necessarily depict *only* White characters, the percentage of characters from diverse backgrounds are as follows: 0.9% American Indian/First Nations; 2.4% Latinx; 3.3% Asian Pacific/Asian Pacific American; 7.6% African/African American; 12.5% animals, trucks, etc.; and 73% White (see Cooperative Children's Book Center, n.d.). The Cooperative Children's Book Center summed up the reality of representation in children books with these words: "White people are not notably, or even noticeably, lacking in books for children and teens." In other words, historically, White children have always had and continue to have an abundance of positive images of self, reflecting at them in the pages of children's books. This has not been the case for non-White children, Black boys especially.

When non-White children do not see themselves reflected in the books they read or when the images are distorted, negative, or laughable, positive messages of self-identity, self-affirmation, self-worth, and value are jeopardized. For this reason, early childhood classrooms must be places where children from culturally, linguistically, and economically diverse backgrounds see authentic, positive, multicultural images of themselves in books. As we discuss later in this chapter, children in general, and Black boys in particular, need books that can serve as "mirrors," "windows," and "sliding glass doors" (Bishop, 1990, p. ix).

The statistics and the opening vignette above show clearly that teachers must heed Black boys' critiques of the curriculum, such as Ryheim's. When children do not see themselves reflected in the curriculum, there is the possibility that they will disengage. That is, they may resort to acting out, which sadly for Black boys results in suspensions and academic underachievement, and contributes to the so-called achievement gap. Of all students, Black boys, including pre-K–3rd-grade Black boys like Ryheim, are most likely to be suspended from school. This practice of suspending almost exclusively Black boys, as we have discussed in Chapters 1 and 2, and the fact that it occurs as early as preschool, is cause for serious pause. The deleterious toll this practice takes on the development of the self-identity (defined later in this chapter) of Black boys so early in their schooling experience is both culturally insensitive and assaultive.

According to the U.S. Department of Education Office for Civil Rights (2016), Black preschoolers represent 19% of students but 45% of suspensions. Compounding disciplinary issues, Black boys tend to have lower literacy rates than other students. For example, nationwide, millions of children entering 4th grade are not considered proficient readers. In 2009, 85% of children from low-income backgrounds who attended high-poverty schools failed to reach a proficient reading level on the National Assessment of Educational Progress reading test. Among 3rd-graders (the end of early childhood) with insufficient reading skills, 74% have a drastically reduced likelihood of graduating from high school. In fact, data from the Early Childhood Longitudinal Study indicate that by age 4, children living in poverty have heard 30 million fewer words than their more affluent peers.

It is important to note here that the "30 Million Word Gap," a study conducted by Hart and Risley (1995, 2011) and cited in the report mentioned above, has been critiqued by some scholars for its small sample size. Their critique calls into question the study's widespread generalizability with regard to children living in poverty. Other scholars have speculated whether this is, yet again, social science research "lay[ing] guilt and blame for the persistent and pervasive achievement gap at the feet of poor, African-American women [and fathers], who in their collective failure to talk to their babies—and to talk to them in ways that approximate middle-class parenting—are responsible for later school failure" (Rashid, 2013, p. 28). Still other scholars, Neuman and Moland (2016), examined the consequences of income segregation (the extent to which families of different incomes live in different neighborhoods) (Bischoff & Reardon, 2014) in relation to children's access to print. Their investigation of six urban neighborhoods (Anacostia, Capitol Hill, Hamtramck, University District, Vermont Square, and Culver City) in three major cities (Washington, DC; Detroit; and Los Angeles) revealed stark disparities in terms of access to print for children and their families living in concentrated poverty. Neuman and Moland (2016) describe such urban neighborhoods as "book deserts," which is analogous to the concept of "food deserts." Like the limited access to healthy foods and options in food deserts, the scarcity of books available to children seriously limits their access to developmentally and age-appropriate reading material. This limited and/or reduced access to books in early childhood has both an immediate and long-term effect on a child's vocabulary, background knowledge, and comprehension skills (Allington et al., 2010). The scarcity of books in these communities seriously constrains opportunities for Black boys like Ryheim who come to school eager and ready to learn. Essentially, book deserts and a paucity of multicultural books contribute to aliteracy—students can read but do not like to read.

Evidence of the impact of these book deserts is reflected in studies reporting that by 4th grade, there are significant gaps in early reading proficiency for children of color, especially Black boys, as compared with White boys (Annie E. Casey Foundation, 2016). Corroborating these data is a report from the Schott Foundation (2012) that documents the graduation rates of Black male students. In 2009–2010, 52% of Black male students in the United States graduated from high school compared with 78% for White, non-Latino students. These data raise questions and concerns about access, opportunity, and structural inequalities that remain in schools and society.

As reported above, these statistics are particularly salient when African American boys are considered. Research that examines the literacy development of African American boys and adolescents reveals a widening gap (Tatum, 2005, 2009). The causes contributing to low levels of literacy for African American boys are as complex and unique as their educational and social–emotional needs, which, unfortunately, many schools are not yet prepared to meet. This lack of preparedness ignores the fact that supporting the school readiness and success of children in general, and Black boys in particular, is a shared and collective responsibility that involves the school, family, and community.

This lack of proficiency in reading contributes to negative life outcomes including, but not limited to, intergenerational poverty, dropping out (pushout), retention, incarceration (school-to-prison pipeline), and more. Given these well-documented realities, it is absolutely critical that early childhood teachers provide African American boys with high-quality, multicultural, and culturally relevant literacy activities to ensure that they have greater access to a high-quality education that reflects their lived experiences and will increase their life outcomes. In so doing, teachers must not only explore the self-identities of Black boys and how these identities develop and manifest in diverse contexts, but also interrogate their own attitudes and beliefs that lead to lowered expectations for these students and undermine their agency (defined later in this chapter) to claim and assert their identities in the classroom context.

This investigation into the identities of Black boys, as well as a critical self-reflection about and interrogation of teacher attitudes and beliefs about this population, has the potential to help teachers explore ways they can leverage the identities of Black boys to inform and shape how they manage the classroom and plan and deliver curriculum and instruction that is multicultural, democratic, and culturally responsive. Ford and Milner (2005) explain "self-reflective instruction" as follows:

> Teachers' self-perception and introspection are central for helping students to succeed academically. An important dimension of this philosophy is that of "knowing thyself." Self-reflective teachers are better positioned to observe, understand, and develop tentative hypotheses about the academic and instructional needs of their students. Minimally, teachers should: (a) be familiar with their own learning and teaching styles; (b) be familiar with their strengths and shortcomings as an instructor, including, for example, subject matter knowledge, and an understanding about student learning and development; and (c) be familiar with their biases, stereotypes, and likes and dislikes about working with gifted students and culturally diverse students [Black boys]. (p. 9)

We argue that, guided by self-reflective instruction, all teachers, and White teachers in particular, must learn how to leverage those out-of-school, "everyday" experiences that are learned and cultivated in the homes and communities of Black boys, and how these experiences shape their self-identities and contribute to agency (Wright et al., 2015).

WHO ARE BLACK BOYS? ENDING DEFICIT-ORIENTED NARRATIVES

There is a harmful, dominant narrative about Black boys that almost exclusively portrays them as unteachable, social problems or deviants, and frightening. These are deficit-oriented depictions, and evidence of them is widespread in the American psyche, imagination, and social science journal articles and mainstream media (Wright, 2017). Investment in these negative stereotypes perpetuates "the fear factor," which serves to justify the need for control and punishment (e.g., zero-tolerance policies). That is, Black boys in particular are more harshly punished for the same behavior than White students (U.S. Department of Education Office for Civil Rights, 2016). This continued (mis)framing of Black boys according to "short-sighted, negative, and inaccurate assumptions" (Knight, 2014, p. 434) reinforces and rein-scribes these kinds of stereotypes in the minds of schools and society. As a result, African American boys fail in school, yet there is little outrage. Has the tendency to frame Black boys in terms of deficits and "broken-ness" (e.g., at risk, disengaged, vulnerable) resulted in a normalized view in the minds of so many that Black boys are synonymous with "bad" boys (Ferguson, 2000)? Such framing renders them as one-dimensional, depleted, and a ruined student population besieged by, and destined for, trouble.

How do we prepare educators to view their Black boys differently? Stated another way, how do teachers develop knowledge and strategies to approach teaching Black boys in ways that remove barriers in order to build on their potential, strengths, and assets? As Ford (2011) noted, the less educators know about Black boys, the more they make up. And the reverse— the more educators know, the less they make up. This is a fundamental belief of the authors and why we have written this book. Answering this question regarding preparation requires that teachers (all educators) end the practice of determining that the school readiness and success of Black boys are based largely on the extent to which they can approximate the ways of talking, thinking, and behaving demonstrated by White children, who frequently have had more access and exposure to mainstream experiences that contribute to their ability to comport themselves in ways that reflect, represent, and enforce the "school's typically unexamined norms of what counts as intellectual work" (Rosebery & Warren, 2001, p. 6). This type of ranking, sorting, and identification of who's ready versus who's not ready for school success, makes invisible the promise, potential, and possibilities that Black boys bring with them into the early childhood classroom. Moreover, it ignores barriers rooted in institutional racism and personal implicit biases that marginalize Black boys. Conversely, when a strengths-based and asset-based approach is taken, African American boys are not thought of as being "at risk," but rather "placed at risk" by the very systems and mindsets that historically have viewed them from a deficit perspective (Boykin, 2013).

THE MORE WE KNOW, THE LESS WE MAKE UP

When an anti-deficit achievement framework (Harper, 2015) is used by schools, negative terms that undermine Black boys' self-identity and agency, such as "too active," "overly aggressive," "average," "at risk," "confused," and "getting into trouble," are changed to positive ways to describe this population, such as "engaging," "lively," "intelligent," "gifted," "talented," "imaginative," and more. Then, these boys are not as much "at risk" as they are "at promise." When educators approach the teaching and learning wants and needs of African American boys from an anti-deficit achievement framework, they structure nurturing, self-identity, and agency-building opportunities through culturally responsive teaching and learning that recognizes the potential, gifts, talents, resiliency, and curiosity of Black boys (Trotman Scott, Wright, & Ford, 2018).

Moving beyond deficit narratives and depressing statistics, which without question require serious conversations and robust interventions, we turn to a focus on fostering among African American boys healthy self-identity and agency that contribute strongly to high academic achievement.

How can teachers engage Black boys in the development of a positive self-identity? To begin answering this question, we turn to the work of Derman-Sparks and Edwards (2010), who state that in their vision of anti-bias education "all children and families have a sense of belonging and experience affirmation of their identities and cultural ways of being" (p. 2). To help African American boys experience self-identity affirmation, we recommend authentic multicultural and culturally responsive children's books that serve as mirrors reflecting the lives of Black boys and men in authentic ways that demonstrate their humanity. When these reflections are distorted and stereotypical, Black boys (and girls) absorb negative messages about themselves and people like them. This does little in the way of developing a healthy self-identity. We deliberately and intentionally combined children's books featuring Black boys as protagonists with social studies in an effort to expose Black boys to "mentors on paper" (Thompson, 1996) that make visible the diversity of experiences and contributions made by Black boys and men in their schools, families, and communities past and present. We want teachers to educate themselves and all of their students, but especially Black boys, using books that reflect positive images of self-identity, agency, and community of Black boys toward empowerment.

SELF-IDENTITY, AGENCY, AND COMMUNITY

Self-identity answers the question, "Who am I?" Who we are distinguishes us from everyone else in the world. Children learn about themselves and construct their own self-identity in the context of their families and communities. Aware that their culture comes from their family, children begin to see themselves as members of a group that distinguishes itself from others (York, 2016). As children experience enculturation (sometimes also referred to as socialization), which refers to a child learning cultural norms and behaviors for the first time, and acculturation, which refers to the learning that occurs when people from different cultures come in contact with one another, they begin "to understand that they are a member of a family, an ethnic culture, a classroom, and a religion, and a citizen of a town, state, and country" (p. 33). This process of self-identity development is influenced by multiple social and cultural factors, and it

> requires viewing each child within the sociocultural context of that child's family, educational setting, and community, as well as within the broader society. These various contexts are interrelated, and all powerfully influence the developing child. For example, even a child in a loving, supportive family within a strong, healthy community is affected by the biases of the larger society, such as racism or sexism, and may show some effects of its negative stereotyping and discrimination. (NAEYC, 2009, p. 13)

Understanding on the part of teachers about how Black boys construct their self-identity, and the extent to which they feel they are important members of their classroom community, with all the rights and privileges afforded other children, not only situates their cultural and personal identities as learners, but also develops agency, empowering their use of everyday experiences learned outside of school to problem solve and better understand their world.

AGENCY AND BLACK BOYS

Agency answers the questions, "What actions can I take?" and "Will my actions make a difference?" Children's ability to act upon their cultural worlds of home and school is one example of agency. Agency is children's ability to construct and co-construct their environment by negotiating different courses of action. For example, when children choose among different learning center activities or negotiate sharing props during dramatic play, they exercise agency by problem solving to satisfy the needs of both individuals and the group (Wright et al., 2015). In the case of Ryheim, he felt empowered to ask his teacher, "How come there ain't no Black boys in these books?"

Building on the story of Ryheim, who lost interest in reading as a 2nd-grader, we explore the development of healthy self-identity and agency in African American boys. This focus is central to this book in part because the early childhood teaching profession is dominated by White women, many of whom, while interested in helping all their students succeed, may lack firsthand experience with Black boys, like the teacher and student teachers introduced in Chapter 2 (Mrs. Kay, Chelsea, and Alice). These teachers need to connect with their Black boys, beyond deficit views. There is the need to figure out how to encourage and motivate the "Ryheims" in the classroom to (re)discover a passion for reading books that are for and about them. This tackles aliteracy and ensures that Black boys remain literate.

In light of the need to encourage and motivate Black boys, we pose another question: "How can early childhood teachers make the curriculum rigorous and culturally relevant to engage the self-identities of Black boys?" The answer to this question is important given legitimate concerns about the need to make curriculum relevant for Black boys (Gay, 2010; Ladson-Billings, 2009; Wright & Ford, 2017b). Such relevance is necessary to support their school readiness and academic success in ways that promote healthy self-identity and encourage their agency in the early childhood classroom. To repeat, Black boys frequently complain about what is presented (or not presented) in the curriculum, viewing it as uninteresting or irrelevant to their interests and lived experiences. The voices, feelings, and perspectives of Black boys often are not respected and valued by their teachers or classmates (Wright et al., 2015). Ford and Milner (2005) assert that "students' comments provide important insights into what must be done to change curriculum and instruction. The students are sending us a clarion call to change—they want their education to be relevant, meaningful, personal, and empowering" (p. 24). This is a reasonable request from our youngest and most impressionable student population.

If education lacks relevance, it becomes meaningless. More specifically, if the curriculum and literature adopted do not engage Black boys toward the development of healthy self-identity, they may lose interest, begin to fail, and, in many cases, be removed from the classroom (i.e., be suspended). This brings us to a discussion of the role that multicultural children's books can play in honoring, affirming, and respecting Black boys as they journey toward the development of a healthy self-identity and agency. We conclude this chapter with a discussion about ways to integrate the Black pride, self-esteem, and agency of Black boys into the curriculum.

MIRROR BOOKS VERSUS WINDOW BOOKS: REFLECTION MATTERS

Teachers and families contribute to African American boys' discovery of who they are—historically, socially, culturally, intellectually, and academically. Designing and implementing a celebration of African American children's literature ensures that Black boys see themselves in books as the protagonist (main character, advocate or champion of a particular cause or idea) and serves to foster healthy self-identity and agency. Moreover, such books are vital to helping teachers build relationships (community) by giving students some control over their self-image.

Black boys, perhaps more than any other group of children, need greater access to what Rudine Sims Bishop coined as "mirror" books. Black boys also need windows and, at times, sliding glass doors in their development of a healthy self-identity and agency. According to Bishop (1990):

> Books are sometimes windows, offering views of worlds that may be real or imagined, familiar or strange. These windows are also sliding glass doors, and

readers have only to walk through in imagination to become part of whatever world has been created and recreated by the author. When lighting conditions are just right, however, a window can also be a mirror. Literature transforms human experience and reflects it back to us, and in that reflection we can see our own lives and experiences as part of the larger human experience. Reading, then, becomes a means of self-affirmation, and readers often seek their mirrors in books. (p. ix)

While it is true that good literature has the potential to be impactful across diverse racial-ethnic groups, non-White children in general, and Black children (as discussed earlier in this Chapter) in particular, have fewer books that reflect their own image. For this reason, we emphasize in this chapter the importance of mirror books. Black boys need to physically see positive images of themselves reflected back at them in children's books. This, we argue, has the potential to become an example of a compelling counter-narrative to the history of the "all-White world" (Larrick, 1965) of children's books that present Black characters only as "objects of ridicule and generally inferior beings" (Bishop, 2012, p. 6). When Black boys see themselves portrayed visually, textually, and realistically in children's books, an important message of recognition, value, affirmation, and validation is conveyed. Moreover, recognition of the sociocultural context in which they live and are growing up is celebrated.

Students' growth as readers depends extensively on their ability to engage with, relate to, and make connections with what they read, as in the case of Ryheim. To avoid the potential of oversimplifying the importance of mirror books, we are not suggesting that simply providing African American boys with books with Black characters, written by Black authors, alone will increase their desire to read and result in healthy self-identity and agency. To achieve the latter, books for and about Black boys must be rigorous, authentic, multicultural, and developmentally appropriate. Multicultural books should introduce children to information about values of justice, fairness, and equity. Books that are developmentally appropriate should vary with and adapt to the age, experience, and interests of Black boys. These stories must expose Black boys to culturally relevant counter-stories—stories that counteract the dominant discourse that has depicted Black boys primarily as "at risk" versus placed at risk, "without hope" versus hopeful, or "out of control and dangerous" (Tatum, 2005, p. 28) versus developing self-control like all other children.

African American children's book writer Elizabeth Fitzgerald Howard (1991) explained the critical need for counter-stories in this way:

We must also aim for that authentic body of literature for children which can lead us toward our goals: self-esteem for those previously not reflected in the mirror, and important enlightenment for those who, for too long, have seen only themselves in that mirror; all leading toward the celebration of living in the multicultural society. (p. 92)

Howard's sentiments are reflected in the 2010 National Council for the Social Studies (NCSS) standards and linked to the NAEYC Standards for Early Childhood Professional Preparation. We draw on NCSS Standard I: Culture; NCSS Standard IV: Individual Development and Identity; and NCSS Standard V: Individuals, Groups, and Institutions.

NATIONAL COUNCIL FOR THE SOCIAL STUDIES STANDARDS

There are 10 NCSS thematic strands; however, for the purposes of this chapter, we focus on only three strands (Standards I, IV, and V). NCSS Standard I: Culture, is the first of the thematic strands. We begin with culture as it serves as an overarching framework. Culture is central to who we are as individuals and as a society. Culture is also what binds and divides us. Thus, understanding and accepting differences and similarities can never come too early in life (Ramsey, 2015; York, 2016). When children start school, they are likely to come into contact with more children from diverse racial, ethnic, linguistic, religious, and economic backgrounds than they have before. Some of these children will be like them, and some will be different. According to *The Condition of Education 2011* (Aud et al., 2011), 52% of births in that year were non-White; these are the students who entered kindergarten in 2016. For these reasons, it is important in these early years, these impressionable years, that teachers develop an understanding of the child's own culture and foster cross-cultural understanding in the early childhood classroom. It is also essential for teachers to resist color-blind and/or culturally assaultive approaches that ignore and undermine the cultural and personal self-identities of students. Culturally responsive "social studies programs should include experiences that provide for the study of culture and cultural diversity" (NCSS, 2010, p. 14). Self-knowledge that ensues from exposure to culturally relevant teaching and learning in a diverse world (see Ramsey, 2015) is an important basis for fostering healthy self-identity and agency in African American boys in democratic learning environments (Wright et al., 2015).

NCSS Standard IV: Individual Development and Identity, focuses on and incorporates a discussion about self and others. NCSS Standard V focuses on self, groups, and institutions. Together, these standards emphasize community and social skills. Attention to community relates to those communities to which we belong, which consist of groups and institutions that have an effect on our development (NCSS, 2010). The ideas and ideals emphasized in both standards relate to the importance of social skills development to enable children to function in diverse groups, communities, and institutions.

To help African American boys experience an affirmation of self-identity, we recommend authentic social studies teaching that celebrates "Black boy joy" through a "History and Me" approach that places Black boys at the center of pedagogy to ensure that their identities are foregrounded (Vasquez, 2014). This approach uses authentic picture books that feature Black boys as the protagonists and is an anti-deficit, culturally responsive approach that reflects, represents, and celebrates the brilliance we believe resides in African American boys. Building on these ideas and ideals, we explore ways to foster healthy self-identity and agency that expose Black boys (and other children) to self-love and that honor historic acts of social change in America with an emphasis on African Americans. Both the "Black boy joy" framing and the "History and Me" approach are deliberate efforts to disrupt "the discourse of controlling *what, how,* and *when* children learn, as well as *who* gets to learn *what,* [which] continues to exist even though there have been many gains at constructing more equitable schooling" (Vasquez, 2014, p. xiii).

ENGAGING BLACK BOYS USING MULTICULTURAL CHILDREN'S LITERATURE

It cannot be emphasized enough that Black boys' opportunities to see themselves as the main characters in children's books, and to reflect on their interests and experiences, are few and far between. We assert that mirror/multicultural books contribute to self-identity and allow Black boys to exercise agency, control their self-image, and build community early in their school experiences. These books portray positive images of Black boys, which are missing from the public's imagination, and inject a voice into the existing dialogue that often is left out—that of Black boys like Ryheim.

Multicultural children's literature ensures that students experience a mirror that reflects their humanity and culture, and honors and celebrates their identities. Educators must ensure that children's literature is a mirror rather than a distortion of human life reflecting nondominant groups. Educators must ensure that Black boys are not exposed solely to window experiences in which they are looking outward at what others are doing, and their own reflection is missing. Failure to select authentic children's literature exposes children, Black boys in particular, to "negative messages about themselves and people like them" (Bishop, 1993, p. 43). When cultural authenticity is missing from children's books, "those who see only themselves or who are exposed to errors and misrepresentations are miseducated into a false sense of superiority, and the harm is doubly done" (p. 43).

In a multicultural curriculum, there are few stimuli with greater potential to move people to action than literature. Because it tells the stories of human events and the human condition and not simply facts, literature does more than change minds; it changes hearts. And people with changed hearts are people who can move the world (Rasinksi & Padak, 1990). In this spirit, we foster healthy self-identity and agency in Black boys by using Ford's (2011) Bloom–Banks Matrix with children's books that are aligned with the aforementioned social studies standards. The Matrix merges rigor and relevance, and can be used to accentuate the self-identities and agency of Black boys as protagonists in authentic multicultural children's books.

In 1999, Ford and Harris created the Bloom–Banks Matrix, a twofold model used to address the need to make learning rigorous and relevant for students. The Matrix blends the best of critical thinking (Anderson et al., 2004; Bloom, 1956) and multicultural curriculum (Banks, 2009) to provide teachers with a tool to develop lessons that offer rigor with substantive multicultural content. In the next sections, we summarize the Matrix and describe how it can be used as a pedagogical tool to foster healthy self-identity and agency, while at the same time increasing rigor and relevance for Black boys in the early childhood classroom.

Banks's Multicultural Curriculum Model: An Overview

In numerous books, James Banks (1994, 2014) has presented a concrete model (Approaches to Integrating Multicultural Content), containing four levels, of how to infuse multicultural content into the curriculum. The four levels are contributions, additive, transformative, and social action. As shown in Figure 4.1, key words have been identified that are useful for remembering the content focus and goals for each level of Banks's Multicultural Curriculum Content Model. The four levels are described below.

1. The **contributions** level is the lowest level and most commonly adopted in schools. It focuses on elements and artifacts with no regard for their meaning, significance, and history. Consequently, the superficiality of these artifacts creates and/or reinforces stereotypes, such as readings and lessons instructing students to make teepees, to create totem poles, to dress as a racially different group or individual, or to bring foods from their culture or the culture of other groups. The most problematic result is the creation or reinforcement of stereotypes and the dehumanization of groups of color.

   Key words for contributions level: food, fun, fashion, folklore

2. The **additive** level is slightly higher than contributions in Banks's model. It focuses on ideas and issues that are safe, with little chance

Figure 4.1. Key Words to Remember When Applying Banks's Multicultural Content Model

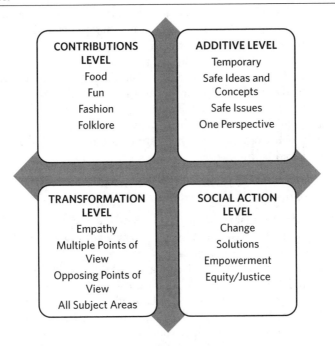

of being controversial. Students talk and read books about sexism and classism, for example, yet they do not read and learn about racism. Students, instead, learn about s/heroes of color who are less controversial (e.g., Dr. Martin Luther King, Jr., versus Malcolm X, or Coretta Scott King versus Angela Y. Davis). (See "Ten Quick Ways to Analyze Children's Books for Sexism and Racism" in *Anti-Bias Curriculum: Tools for Empowering Young Children* [Derman-Sparks & A.B.C. Task Force, 1989].) Lessons and readings are an add-on that is not integral to the curriculum, such as Black History Month and Hispanic Heritage Month. Consequently, students acquire a superficial, polemic, tangential understanding of groups of color being studied.

Key words for additive level: *temporary, safe ideas and concepts, safe issues, one perspective*

3. The third level is ***transformation***, whereby teachers endeavor to transform the curriculum in regard to ideas, concepts, themes, issues, and topics in all subject areas. Controversial topics are not avoided; social ills and inequities are addressed. This level is rigorous. Students

are exposed to many points of view and to opposing perspectives, making it nonpolemic (as it was at the additive level). In promoting multiple points of view, teachers ideally help students become critical thinkers, developing critical literacy skills that go beyond simply learning to read and write, to include the motivation and capacity to be critical of what they read, see, and hear, and to probe beyond superficial understanding and to question common wisdom and whitewashed materials. Also important is that students are given opportunities to become empathetic, by being encouraged to put themselves in the position of those facing challenges (e.g., How would you feel if you were the Black boy in the children's book *Chocolate Me?* discussed below).

Key words for transformation level: empathy, multiple points of view, opposing points of view, all subject areas

4. The *social action* level is the highest in Banks's model. At this level, student learning is based on lessons and activities that provide experiences with transformation. Students are encouraged and enabled to make recommendations for change to improve issues and problems; if opportunity permits, they act upon those recommendations. The goal is to empower students (e.g., Black boys) to envision and seek change for the betterment of their own lives and the lives of others, their community, and the larger society.

Key words for social action level: change, solutions, empowerment, equity/justice (Ford, Wright, Grantham, & Moore, 2018)

Bloom's Taxonomy: Critical Thinking, Creative Thinking, and Problem Solving

Bloom's Taxonomy of Educational Objectives provides instructional rigor—critical thinking, creative thinking, and problem solving. When teachers utilize the six-level cognitive domains, they are able to determine Black boys' ability or skills to recall basic and factual information (knowledge/knowing); understand and explain what was learned (comprehension/understanding); apply and use what was learned (application/applying); form views, predict, and compare–contrast information (analysis/analyzing); study, judge/critique, and support what was taught and learned (evaluation/evaluating); and use what was taught and learned to develop new, original, and/or improved products (synthesis/creating).

Lessons and literature lack rigor if students are not given the opportunity to think critically and act accordingly, guided by a sense of equity and social justice (i.e., working to create a society with equitable distribution of resources and opportunities). The curriculum must allow students, in this case, Black boys, to see themselves positively reflected in literature and the curriculum (e.g., social studies) and as potential agents of change.

The Bloom–Banks Matrix: An Overview

The Bloom–Banks Matrix (Ford, 2011; Ford & Harris, 1999) combines Bloom's taxonomy (Anderson et al., 2004; Bloom, 1956) and Banks's (2009) model to create a model that reflects the goals, objectives, and perspectives of differentiation that encompasses rigor and relevance. The result of the merger is a 4-quadrant matrix that consists of 24 cells (see Figure 4.2, following spread). The Matrix fits well with NCSS Standards I, IV, and V due to the mutual focus on culture and identity. The lowest cell level in the matrix is knowledge–contributions and the highest and most rigorous cell is social action–synthesis.

Quadrant 1: Lessons presented in this quadrant are low on both Bloom's taxonomy and Banks's multicultural model. Teachers commonly provide lessons from the six cells in this quadrant. However, when lessons are low on Bloom's taxonomy (knowledge, comprehension, and application) *and* low on Banks's multicultural levels (contributions and additive), there is a high likelihood that the content will not be challenging or interesting for Black boys (Ford, 2011).

Quadrant 2: Lessons in this quadrant are high on Bloom's taxonomy (analysis, evaluation, and synthesis) but low on Banks's multicultural levels (contributions and additive). These lessons allow Black boys to use their critical thinking, creativity, and problem-solving skills, but multicultural content is superficial or presented in stereotypical ways. Assignments in this quadrant challenge Black boys cognitively, but substantive (authentic, responsive) multicultural content will be missing. This quadrant is most commonly used when teachers are familiar with Bloom but not Banks (Ford, 2011).

Quadrant 3: Lessons in this quadrant are low on Bloom's taxonomy (knowledge, comprehension, and application) but high on Banks's multicultural levels (transformation and social action). Lesson plans in these six cells allow Black boys to elaborate on events, facts, and characteristics of culturally different groups; this will help them become more aware and gain additional and meaningful knowledge about different groups, issues, concepts, and themes. Black boys will be given opportunities to view cultural events, concepts, and themes through the lens and lives of others. However, this quadrant is considered guarded because although social action may take place, it does not require critical thinking and problem solving. When developing lessons, teachers may be familiar with Bloom's taxonomy regarding

Figure 4.2. Ford's Bloom–Banks Matrix: Cell Definitions

	Knowledge	Comprehension	Application	Analysis	Evaluation	Synthesis
Contributions	Students are taught and know facts about cultural artifacts, events, groups, and other cultural elements.	Students show an understanding of information about cultural artifacts, groups, etc.	Students are asked to and can apply information learned about cultural artifacts, events, etc.	Students are taught to and can analyze (e.g., compare and contrast) information about cultural artifacts, groups, etc.	Students are taught to and can evaluate facts and information based on cultural artifacts, groups, etc.	Students are required to and can create a new product from the information on cultural artifacts, groups, etc.
Additive	Students are taught and know concepts and themes about cultural groups.	Students are taught and can understand cultural concepts and themes.	Students are required to and can apply information learned about cultural concepts and themes.	Students are taught to and can analyze important cultural concepts and themes.	Students are taught to and can critique and evaluate cultural concepts and themes.	Students are asked to and can synthesize important information about cultural concepts and themes.

Transformation	Students are given information on important cultural elements, groups, etc., and can understand this information from different perspectives.	Students are taught to understand and can demonstrate an understanding of important cultural concepts and themes from different perspectives.	Students are asked to and can apply their understanding of important concepts and themes from different perspectives.	Students are taught to and can examine important cultural concepts and themes from more than one perspective.	Students are taught to and can critique, evaluate, or judge important cultural concepts and themes from different viewpoints (e.g., minority group).	Students are required to and can create a product based on their new perspective or the perspective of another group.
Social Action	Based on information about cultural artifacts, etc., students make recommendations for social action.	Based on their understanding of important concepts and themes, students make recommendations for social action.	Students apply their understanding of important social and cultural issues; they also make recommendations and take action on these issues.	Students are required to and can analyze social and cultural issues from different perspectives; they take action on these issues.	Students critique important social and cultural issues, and seek to make change.	Students create a plan of action to address a social and/or cultural issue(s); they seek change.

Source: Ford (2011).

critical thinking but not familiar with Banks's multicultural model, which integrates multicultural content in a culturally responsive way (Ford, 2011).

Quadrant 4: High on Bloom's taxonomy (analysis, evaluation, and synthesis) *and* Banks's multicultural levels (transformation and social action), this quadrant provides Black boys with opportunities to think critically, solve problems, and review a multitude of multicultural topics, issues, and themes. Importantly, students suggest or make recommendations for social change. Lessons in this quadrant are both rigorous *and* relevant. Hence, Black boys will be able to think and solve problems at the highest levels, while being exposed to content that validates them individually and as a group. This is the ideal quadrant for all students (Ford, 2011) and aligns with NCSS Standards I, IV, and V.

The Matrix is useful in all educational settings, ranging from gifted to mixed-ability to special education classrooms. It is also useful in all demographic settings from predominantly White classrooms to racially diverse classrooms to predominantly Black classrooms. When using the Matrix, teachers are able to teach the same content at differing levels and allow all students, specifically Black boys, to experience meaning and success on levels and in ways that meet their needs and interests as individuals and community members. All students have the right to be educated using rigorous *and* relevant lessons, materials, and literature. Black boys are no exception; more must be supported to reach their potential. We agree with the United Negro College Fund—a mind is a terrible thing to waste—and with Ford (2010) that a mind is a terrible thing to erase.

AUTHENTIC CHILDREN'S BOOKS PROMOTE SELF-IDENTITY AND AGENCY

As previously discussed, self-identity answers a fundamental question, "Who am I?" Agency answers the questions, "What actions can I take?" and "Will my actions make a difference?" Children's ability and efficacy to act upon their cultural worlds of home and school is just one example of agency. Guided by these questions of self-identity and agency, we have chosen two books that focus on self-identity, and two books that focus on agency (see Figure 4.3). Together, these selected books illustrate self-identity and agency in Black boys.

Before we discuss each book using the Bloom–Banks Matrix, it is important to note that picture books featuring Black boys as protagonists do not alone accomplish self-identity, agency, a sense of belonging, and/or affirmation for African American boys. Although absolutely critical, as mentioned before, not only is it about how Black boys like Ryheim relate

Figure 4.3. Selected Books That Promote Self-Identity and Agency

Title, Author, Date	Book Summary
Chocolate Me by Taye Diggs; illustrations by Shane W. Evans (2011)	The boy is teased for looking different from the other kids. His skin is darker, his hair curlier. He tells his mother he wishes he could be more like everyone else. And she helps him to see how beautiful he really, truly is.
I'm A Brilliant Little Black Boy! by Joshua B. Drummond and Betty K. Bynum; illustrations by Brian McGee (2016)	Joshua learns that through studying, good deeds, working hard, and aiming to be brilliant . . . we can really shine!
Jamal's Busy Day by Wade Hudson; illustrations by George Ford (1991)	Jamal is making preparations for school that his parents make to begin their day. Parents and child can work hard and accomplish a lot.
Ron's Big Mission by Rose Blue and Corinne Naden; illustrations by Don Tate (2009)	Nine-year-old Ron loves going to the library to look through all the books on airplanes and flight. Ron is ready to take out books by himself. But in segregated South Carolina in the 1950s, he cannot. This is his first courageous mission.

to books where they "see themselves, their culture, and their perspectives" (McNair, 2014, p. 69) represented, but, as Tatum explained,

> African American males need exposure to texts which not only contain characters who look, act, and think as they do, but texts which encourage and empower these young men to take action in their own lives and in the lives of others around them. (as cited in Hughes-Hassell, Kumasi, Rawson, & Hitson, 2012, p. 6)

He further explained that part of the reason why African American boys

> suffer academically, emotionally, and culturally is a lack of exposure to texts that they find meaningful and that will help them critique, understand, and move beyond some of the turmoil-related experiences they encounter outside school. (as cited in Hughes-Hassell et al., 2012, p. 6)

We, too, assert that the responsibility is not on Black boys alone to "move beyond" the manufactured and systemic racially motivated inequalities that so many encounter as early as preschool. Children should not have to navigate racism and discrimination. Unfortunately, however, because childhoods are unequal (see Lareau, 2011), Black boys, as early as preschool, find themselves faced with stereotypes that erase their childhood innocence, resulting in their persistent criminalization and adultification. This, unfortunately, is also true for Black girls as early as 5 years of age (see Epstein et al., 2017). As one way of eliminating such stigmatization toward healthy self-identity and agency, we recommend the use of what Tatum refers to as "enabling texts." Such texts do the following:

- promote a healthy psyche
- reflect an awareness of the real world
- focus on the collective struggle of African Americans
- serve as a roadmap for being, doing, thinking, and acting (Tatum, 2009, as cited in Hughes-Hassell et al., 2012, p. 6)

Contextualizing the above assertions, we contend that Black boys must have opportunities to discuss these books with their teachers and classmates and to participate in a variety of activities (such as pantomime, choral readings, readers' theater, mask making, puppetry, storytelling, and improvisation) (Gangi, 2004; Rasinski, 2010). These "mirror books" or "mentors on paper" (Thompson, 1996) ideally should contribute to intellectual growth, agency, voice, identity, resilience, resolve, and a positive life trajectory for Black boys.

When discussing these books with children, it is essential to remember that context and lived experiences matter. The ways in which we have mapped out each story in terms of the setting (Where? When?), characters (Who?), problem (What is the main issue or challenge?) (i.e., good or bad), and solution (How is the problem solved?) are intentional, as our primary purpose is to represent, reflect, promote, and foreground for teachers how to foster healthy self-identity and agency to motivate, engage, and celebrate Black boys. Literature and curriculum should and must not be decontextualized. That is, the curriculum and children's books used to foster self-identity and agency cannot be devoid of the individual and collective experiences of Black boys. Also, such a focus on self-identity and agency should and must not be treated as an "add-on" that is tangential to the curriculum, but instead should be treated as central to the curriculum. We are not there yet. Because of the extent to which Black boys have been disadvantaged by the schooling context, it is necessary to counteract, by honoring their experiences in positive ways, the persistent and pervasive inequities and injustices that arise frequently in their lives inside and outside of school. And this practice is long overdue. Therefore, what we argue herein is that this frame and/or perspective should drive the focus on Black boys as a deliberate attempt to disrupt problematic, inequitable ways that are not engaging this student population.

Guided by this charge, the examples from each text that we have chosen to highlight should serve as points of departure for how to foster healthy self-identity and agency in Black boys. We realize that the fidelity of applying the Bloom–Banks Matrix to promote self-identity and agency through the use of authentic multicultural children's books will depend on the cultural competence of the teacher and the context in which the Matrix is used. Adopting these books requires critical literacy—the desire, attitudes, skills, and ability to disrupt, critique, and think deeply about texts. This, then, will lead to a long-needed proactive and productive redesign of those problematic ways of framing Black boys from deficit-oriented perspectives. We advocate for and urge that teachers move toward the creation of a counternarrative of Black boys not being "at risk" but "at promise." Achieving these aims requires teachers to research and understand how policies (e.g., school discipline, referrals to gifted education) and institutions like schools mis-position Black boys in disadvantaged ways. Central, therefore, to this critical examination is unpacking the relationship between teachers in general, White teachers, and White female teachers (the majority of the profession), with regard to Black boys.

What follows are details from four matrices used to analyze books for and about Black boys in positive, affirming, motivating, and culturally responsive ways. The matrices are presented in Figures 4.4, 4.5, 4.6, and 4.7 at the end of this chapter. In common with Bishop (1990), we advocate for providing all children, especially children (boys) of color, the opportunity to encounter literature that resonates with them. We want Black boys to be neither illiterate (e.g., unable to read) nor aliterate (i.e., unwilling to read). We begin with *Chocolate Me*.

Chocolate Me. This book, written by actor Taye Diggs, is about a Black boy who is teased for looking different. His skin is darker, his hair curlier than his friends' (Timmy, Johnny, and Mark), who happen to be White boys. The Black boy is teased for the color of his skin ("It's brown like dirt. Does it hurt to wash off?"), the shape of his nose, the texture of his hair, and the brightness of his teeth. Consequently, he wishes he could be more like his friends in order to "fit" in. He shared his wish with his mother, who quickly introduces a counter-narrative to counteract the negative messages. Through a series of positive messages (e.g., "You have skin like velvet fudge frosting mixed in a bowl. . . . Cotton candy hair soft to the touch of my fingertips"), his mother helps him realize that he is beautiful. The positive messages from his mother empower him toward the end of the story to celebrate all those things that make him unique. Figure 4.4 provides ways teachers can engage their students, especially Black boys, in a discussion of this book so as to foster healthy self-identity and agency.

How does *Chocolate Me* support self-identity? This book can serve a variety of purposes in the early childhood classroom, especially with regard to children's development of a positive self-concept and self-esteem. Children in the primary grades begin comparing themselves with their peers, as the Black boy in this story does when he says to his mother, "Why can't

I be more like Timmy or Johnny or Mark with straight hair and a different nose?" The boy's desire to be like his friends is common among school-aged children, who tend to describe themselves in terms of their characteristics, traits, and abilities.

Helping young children accept, value, and celebrate their diverse characteristics, traits, and abilities, while encouraging them to explore new ways of knowing and being in the world, should and must be an important part of every early childhood classroom. The boy's mother encourages her son to see his outer beauty when she says, "Look in the mirror and love what you see!" Like the boy's mother, teachers must help children see their outer and inner beauty. Moreover, teachers must not view teasing and/or bullying as a typical part of a child's development. This view not only compromises harmony in a democratic class, but it jeopardizes a child's well-being.

Chocolate Me can serve as an authentic children's book to foster Black boys' healthy self-identity. Experiences in the early grades that shape self-identity and agency are especially important for Black boys because of how much those experiences influence their behavior. Since the book counteracts with positive messages the myriad ways in which the labeling of Black boys as "bad boys" or "troublemakers" affects their experiences in and outside of school, *Chocolate Me* can serve as a starting point to talk about what it means to feel different, why differences are important, and why acceptance of others along lines of race, class, gender, ability, and disability is important to building racial and cultural awareness and competence in all children.

As a result of the mother's counter-narrative to counteract the negative messages from the boy's friends, he realizes they are wrong. While the author does not mention that the boy's friends apologize, teachers can highlight the importance of the development of emotional understanding and empathy, which is a process for young children. By this, we mean that teachers can help children understand that part of the ability to maintain relationships with friends and classmates is the ability to infer feelings and points of view. While much has been written in child development about children's egocentric perspectives, with scaffolding children eventually can understand the feelings of others. Helping children empathize with others can lead to acceptance, such as, "I believe each person is special and unique."

It is important to note here that the authors debated the inclusion of *Chocolate Me* in this chapter as an example of how to foster healthy self-identity because of some of the negative reviews from the general public posted on the Internet. At the time of this writing, there were 115 reviews posted on the www.goodreads.com website. Here are just a few of the verbatim comments about the book: "This is a tough book" (posted December 7, 2012), "I feel this book can be considered racist" (posted November 3, 2011), "I cannot ever imagine reading this book to a group of students" (posted May 13, 2012), "Read this for Black History Month Story Time!"

(posted February 15, 2015), "This [is] a great book, while many think it's racist by the words it is not. Quite honestly it speaks [to] the harsh realities about African American children who grow up around children of different ethnicities" (posted June 22, 2016). The trepidation surrounding talking about "race" with very young children left us rethinking what we know about the importance of not shying away from controversial and/or challenging content. As captured in the work of York (2016):

> Racism is a social condition that affects our personal lives, as well as the society at large. During childhood, racism affects our social and emotional development. Without our even knowing it, racism shapes our personal and racial identity, and it shapes our experience in the US society. Children learn social roles and become members of US society through the process known as socialization. Unfortunately, by growing up in the United States, we have been socialized to take our place in a racist society. (p. 59)

To ignore the impact of racism on children's development is to ignore what we know about children's identity and attitude development, and research data by Derman-Sparks (2008) that reveals the following:

- Children begin to notice differences and construct classificatory and evaluative categories very early.
- Societal stereotyping and bias influence children's self-concept and attitudes toward others. (p. 7)

Together, both poignant quotes challenge the discomfort captured in some of the comments that seem to suggest that just mentioning race in a children's book is racist. This view, in many ways, trivializes and undermines the complexity of racial injury in this country and the assumption made by many adults that children are unaffected by the biases in U.S. society.

We imagine there will be teachers who may be uncomfortable reading this book to their students because, like some of the reviewers, they believe a focus on race is inappropriate for young children. Therefore, we recommend the works of Louise Derman-Sparks and Julie Olsen Edwards (2010), Patricia Ramsey (2015), Susan Neuman and Naomi Moland (2016), and Stacey York (2016) to support our belief about the responsibility of early childhood educators to find ways to prevent and counter these developing attitudes and beliefs *before* they become too deeply ingrained. We also caution against the view that talking about race will make matters worse. To those teachers concerned about this, we offer these words: "It is not differences in themselves that cause the problem, but how people respond to differences" (Derman-Sparks & A.B.C. Task Force, 1989, p. 6).

Ignoring the unequalness of childhoods underestimates what children know and understand about topics of race, class, gender, ability, and/or disability. The fidelity of anti-bias curriculum addresses the importance of engaging young children in discussions about differences, as well as similarities, toward deeper critical conversations about cultural heritages, and struggles of groups and individuals to gain equality and justice.

The authors decided that *Chocolate Me* would not be excluded because of its reference to "race" in an effort to appease those who have chosen to underestimate the power of societal influences or because they have come to believe that a "colorblind" approach is best when it comes to young children and the topic of race. As has been the assertion throughout this book, shying away from difficult and/or controversial content to avoid making our readers uncomfortable would ignore the ways in which race and gender continue to circumscribe the experiences of Black boys both in and outside of school. In the sections that follow, we discuss three other children's books that focus on Black boys.

I'm a Brilliant Little Black Boy! This is a book, written by Joshua B. Drummond and his mother Betty K. Bynum, about a Black boy named Joshua. He has big dreams and ideas that are described as brilliant as the stars. With all his good friends, Joshua's days are filled with adventures with books, a telescope, a red superhero cape, rhyming hip-hop verse, twinkling fireflies that light up the magical summer skies above a cardboard fort in the park—and so much more; this is just what Black boy joy, innocence, and imagination are all about. Kind, smart, creative, and always thinking, Joshua learns that through studying, good deeds, working hard, and aiming to be brilliant . . . we can really shine!

The Bloom–Banks Matrix in Figure 4.5 provides ways for teachers to engage an entire class in a lively discussion about the adventures of the main character as he discovers his different talents, to serve as motivation for Black boys to discover their own gifts and talents.

How can teachers use the book *I'm a Brilliant Little Black Boy!* to foster healthy self-identity in Black boys? The title alone is a departure from "bad boy" and "troublemaker," often used to describe Black boys. As the Matrix outlines, teachers can build on the importance of the use of positive adjectives like *brilliant* to describe Black boys. The positive and constructive messages in the book about Black boys contribute to self-esteem and self-identity. Teachers should highlight how Joshua, a curious little boy, uncovers his intellectual aptitude and creativity with the help of many in his social network. Teachers also can help their students understand that who we are, and who we potentially can become, is as a result of a large group of people that include, but are not limited to, parents/family, friends, teachers, and the community.

In the book, Joshua discovers his multiple identities that build his confidence in his abilities. He discovers painting and astrology, for example. Like the book's authors, teachers can foster in Black boys a sense of cultural pride, and build their self-esteem and self-confidence, toward a healthy self-identity. Finally, teachers can use this book to encourage Black boys to explore their interests, leading to success.

Jamal's Busy Day, discussed next, is yet another book to encourage Black boys to explore their interests and possibilities.

Jamal's Busy Day. This book, written by Wade Hudson, is about a Black boy named Jamal who is an only child. His parents are active, serious professionals—father is an architect and mother is an accountant. In its own way, Jamal's day is as demanding as his parents'. Jamal works with numbers in math class, conducts research in the library, has a meeting to attend in the school auditorium, and settles schoolyard disagreements between his friends. The message is that both parents and children can work hard to accomplish their goals. The Matrix provides ways teachers can engage their students in a discussion of this book, with particular attention given to self-identity and agency. Keeping in mind the NCSS standards, how to foster healthy self-identity and agency is outlined in Figure 4.6, which provides ways teachers can engage their students, especially Black boys, in rigorous discussions on similarities between school and work.

Teachers can use this book to foster healthy self-identity and agency in Black boys by first highlighting all the ways in which Jamal is a happy boy who is involved in a variety of school-related activities. Like his parents, Jamal is a hard worker. Teachers can draw parallels between Jamal and their students and can encourage Black boys to explore all the ways that they are like Jamal. The way in which Jamal takes initiative (agency) is another quality to encourage in Black boys.

We also see initiative (agency) in *Ron's Big Mission* when the title character works to change a discriminatory policy at his local library.

Ron's Big Mission. This book, written by Rose Blue and Corinne Naden, is based on the true story of Dr. Ronald E. McNair, NASA astronaut (deceased), and how he desegregated his library. The setting is South Carolina in the 1950s at a time when African Americans were forbidden to have their own library card. Ron, who was 9 years old at the time, loved books, and when he visited the library he always looked for books with images of children who looked like him (as did Ryheim). However, finding mirror books was a challenge for Ron. Because he could not find a lot of books about Black children, he began to read books about airplanes and space.

Although Ron loved going to the library, he wanted to read his books at home. However, he could not because of the rule that prevented African Americans from having a library card. Ron did not like this rule and decided to do something about it. The book tells of how Ron takes a stand against this discrimination that results in his receiving his very own library card. The library where Ron got his library card is now dedicated to him. How to foster healthy self-identity and agency is outlined in Figure 4.7, which provides ways teachers can engage their students, especially Black boys, in a discussion of this book.

Ron's Big Mission fosters healthy self-identity and agency in Black boys by highlighting a Black boy who likes to read and who makes a difference in his community. Drawing attention to Ron's love of books and reading can motivate students, Black boys especially, who may choose not to read because, like Ryheim in the opening vignette, they do not see themselves reflected in the books made available to them. Pointing out to students that they have the ability to solve problems in their community can be empowering. Teachers can encourage Black boys to imagine what they would do (agency) in Ron's place and to explain how they would solve the problems presented. Teachers can even ask students to consider what they think Ron's life would have been like if he had not stood up for himself. This example of agency can empower all children, but especially Black boys.

CONCLUSION

The analyses of the four selected books using the Bloom–Banks Matrix provide a way of critically engaging students in discussions about characters who are similar to and different from themselves. These books also accentuate "Black boy joy" through enabling texts that promote a healthy psyche, reflect an awareness of the real world, focus on the collective struggle of African Americans, and serve as a roadmap for being, doing, thinking, and acting (Tatum, 2009). These enabling texts can foster healthy self-identity and agency in Black boys, as they reflect awareness of the world while highlighting multiple identities of Black boys both in and outside of school. For instance, these books emphasize the ways Black boys are just like other children—they enjoy school when it affirms their identities, they participate in a variety of activities, they are problem-solvers, and they act in ways that make a difference in their communities.

Accentuating the voices and humanizing the experiences of Black boys with the same level of childhood innocence and protection afforded White children is a key step in addressing the disparate treatment of this young population academically and socially. The prevalence of the adultification of Black boys—that is, the perception that this population is more adult-like and therefore less innocent and not deserving of protection afforded White boys of the same age—must stop if this population is to have the right to be children and the right to a childhood uninterrupted by differential treatment based on race.

A study conducted by Goff and colleagues (2014) found that Black children were likely to be treated differently from White children based solely on race. As discussed early on in this book, Goff and colleagues "found that black boys can be seen as responsible for their actions at an age when White boys still benefit from the assumption that children are essentially innocent" (as cited in Bump, 2014, p. 2). With the average overestimation of age for Black boys exceeding 4½ years, they are misperceived as legal adults at roughly the age of 13. According to Goff and colleagues, at every year after the age of 10, Black boys were considered less innocent than either White or unspecified children. The age of the loss of innocence and protection for Black girls is even earlier. A recent study conducted by Epstein et al. (2017) revealed that adults view Black girls as less innocent and more adult-like than their White peers, at as early as 5 years of age. These findings are profoundly troubling and support research that we have cited elsewhere in this book regarding the role of race, stereotypes, perceptions of innocence, and the loss thereof for Black children in general (and Black boys especially) long before they begin adolescence and reach adulthood.

Because of these and other troubling statistics, we urge those who educate Black boys to interrogate their own attitudes, beliefs, and practices in order to transform the way they think, talk about, and engage the self-identities of Black boys, as well as support and encourage their agency. A needed agenda must acknowledge that, like all other children, Black boys need, want, and deserve to be nurtured. They need, want, and deserve to be protected, supported, comforted, and celebrated. Promoting healthy self-identity and agency in Black boys like Ryheim will have far-reaching implications for reducing the stigmatization of this population, which in large part has resulted in the disproportionate rates of punitive and harsher treatment of them as preschoolers. Approaches that emphasize Black boys' strengths and assets rather than problems or deficits can serve as compelling evidence that "we know boys," and they, in turn, can begin to know themselves.

Figure 4.4. Bloom–Banks Matrix Applied to *Chocolate Me*

	Knowledge/ Knowing	Comprehension/ Understanding	Application/ Applying	Analysis/ Analyzing	Evaluation/ Evaluating	Synthesis/ Creating
Contributions	Where does the story take place? When does the story take place? Who are the main characters?	Explain why the Black boy in the story is not happy. In your own words, explain the title of the book *Chocolate Me*.	Give an example of teasing in the story.	The Black boy does not have a name. Give him a name. Why did the author not give him a name?	Interview at least one classmate about a time when he or she was teased.	Create a poster that promotes acceptance among children.
Additive	What do you like about the book *Chocolate Me*?	Why is the teasing by Timmy, Johnny, and Mark hurtful to the Black boy? Explain in your own words the meaning of teasing. What other words also describe teasing?	Draw a self-portrait and write a sentence that celebrates your name, the color of your skin, the texture of your hair (e.g., curly, straight, thick, thin), the size of your nose, and your teeth.	Do you think Timmy, Johnny, and Mark will apologize after eating the chocolate cupcakes? Make a prediction.	What is similar and different about you and your classmates? How does this affect your friendship? Why do you think Timmy, Johnny, and Mark should apologize to the Black boy? Explain.	Create an "All About Me" poster and/or "I Am Black, I Am Unique" poster.

Transformation	What do Timmy, Johnny, and Mark say about the Black boy? What does the Black boy say when he is teased? Do the bullies seem to care?	Why is it important to celebrate yourself as a Black boy? Why is it not good for children to tease other children about their skin color, hair texture, size of nose, and teeth?	Make a Venn diagram of how you compare with the Black boy in the book *Chocolate Me.*	Do you agree with the Black boy's mother that his skin is like velvet fudge frosting, his hair soft like cotton candy? If yes, explain. If no, explain why not.	Have you ever teased or bullied someone? Why? How do you think he or she felt? Turn and talk to a classmate and ask what he or she likes about him- or herself.	How does the Black boy use his mother's celebration of his skin color, hair texture, nose, and teeth to change his view of himself?
Social Action	Share/read the book with a parent, caregiver, sister, brother, cousin, or friend. Discuss what you learned and listen to what they learned.	If you saw a classmate being teased, what would you do?	Make a list of classroom rules about not teasing and bullying.	Talk to a parent, caregiver, sister, brother, cousin, or friend about why it is not okay to tease other children.	Study the different and varied skin tones, hair textures, and eye color, etc., in the world to promote pride in one's heritage.	Create an "All About Me" poster to be placed in the cafeteria. Use pictures of diverse students to promote the importance of being "proud to be me."

Matrix design adapted from Ford (2011). The authors recommend that teachers be mindful of and sensitive to engaging students in self-identity discussions that include skin color (race). It is important not to embarrass students, which would be culturally insensitive and assaultive. We recommend that teachers read the work of York (2016).

Figure 4.5. Bloom–Banks Matrix Applied to *I'm A Brilliant Little Black Boy!*

	Knowledge/ Knowing	Comprehension/ Understanding	Application/ Applying	Analysis/ Analyzing	Evaluation/ Evaluating	Synthesis/ Creating
Contributions	What is the setting—where does the story take place? When does the story take place? Who is the main character?	How does Joshua's story begin? What is he sharing and talking about?	Make a list of the things that Joshua enjoys doing.	What do Joshua and the stars have in common? What do Joshua and the word *brilliant* have in common?	Interview at least one classmate about his or her favorite subject in school. Why is this his or her favorite subject? What patterns do you see?	Create a graph of favorite school days, activities, and classes.
Additive	What do you want to do for a career/work when you grow up? What does a volcano do? How does it influence nature? What does an artist do?	In what ways is Joshua a brilliant Black boy? What does Joshua mean when he says, "Some days, I like to speak my mind"? What do you like to speak about?	Write a poem (free verse) set to your favorite song as one way to express your feelings.	The author uses the word/ adjective *brilliant* to describe Joshua. What other terms/ adjectives could the author use to describe this boy? What words/ adjectives do you like to use?	What do you want to be when you grow up? Research the requirements. Research the purpose of telescopes and the careers or hobbies they are used in. What does an astrophysicist do?	How does Joshua use his imagination when he wears his red cape? What else could he have used besides a cape?

Transformation	What do you like about Joshua's brilliance as a Black boy? What other smart Black boys do you know?	If you had to explain/justify why you think Joshua is brilliant to your friends, what examples would you use?	Have you ever had a friend or classmate stand up for you? How did you feel?	Make a Venn diagram of how Joshua is similar and different compared with you as a Black boy.	Why do children bully others for getting good grades? How does it make them feel? Interview two or three classmates.	Create a poster or organize a classroom campaign on why doing well in school is important for going to college and choosing careers.
Social Action	Share/read the book with a parent, caregiver, sister, brother, cousin, or friend. Talk with this person about dreams and job/career decisions.	If/when you saw a classmate being bullied for being "brilliant," what would or did you do? Share a few suggestions to help others.	Make a list of classroom rules about supporting others who are doing well.	Why would bullies do this? Share your anti-bully plan with the teacher.	With your group, survey classmates about their thoughts on teasing/bullying to create your own anti-bullying hashtag.	Create a career hashtag and share it in your school. Do a morning announcement and/or skit for the school about the importance of doing well in school in order to go to college and ultimately find a good job.

Matrix design adapted from Ford (2011).

Figure 4.6. Bloom–Banks Matrix Applied to *Jamal's Busy Day*

	Knowledge/ Knowing	Comprehension/ Understanding	Application/ Applying	Analysis/ Analyzing	Evaluation/ Evaluating	Synthesis/ Creating
Contributions	What do Jamal's parents do for a living? What are their jobs?	How does Jamal's day begin?	What are examples of a healthy breakfast? Share a list of food items.	What do Jamal and his mother have in common? What do Jamal and his father have in common?	Interview at least one classmate about his or her career goals.	Create a menu for a healthy breakfast.
Additive	What does an architect do? What does an accountant do? What are their responsibilities?	Why is breakfast important?	Make a timeline showing Jamal's day and compare it with your busy day.	Do you think Jamal will become an accountant or an architect? Make a prediction.	What do you want to be when you grow up? Study/research the career/job requirements.	How does Jamal use his imagination about school and work? Think of more examples of how school and work are similar.

Transformation	Social Action
What do you like about math? Why is math important for being an accountant or architect?	Read the book to a sister, brother, cousin, or friend. If you saw a classmate being bullied, what would you do?
There are not a lot of Black male teachers. Would you like to be one? Would you like to have a Black male teacher?	Talk to your principal about why you or other Black boys would like to have a Black male teacher.
Make a Venn diagram of how Jamal compares school with work. Add more ideas of your own.	Make a list of classroom rules about anti-bullying. Share the list with your teacher, school counselor, and/or principal.
Do you agree with Jamal that school is similar to work? Explain your point of view.	Talk to a sister, brother, cousin, or friend about the importance of doing well in school.
Interview two teachers about why they chose this career. What is similar and different?	Study the school's breakfast or lunch menu. Make at least two suggestions to make it healthier.
Create a flyer showing how school and jobs are either similar or different.	Create an anti-bullying poster to be placed in the cafeteria; use pictures of diverse students.

Matrix design adapted from Ford (2011).

Figure 4.7. Bloom–Banks Matrix Applied to *Ron's Big Mission*

	Knowledge/ Knowing	Comprehension/ Understanding	Application/ Applying	Analysis/ Analyzing	Evaluation/ Evaluating	Synthesis/ Creating
Contributions	Who is the main character? What did Ron want to be when he grew up? What sport did Ron love to play? Where does the story take place?	How does Ron's day begin? How do you begin your day?	List a few examples about a time when you had something important to do like Ron.	What do you think made Ron the head librarian's favorite customer? Do you agree?	How do you think Ron felt when he could not find books in the library about Black kids?	Create a list of how you feel when you find books in the library about Black kids and kids from other racial/ ethnic/cultural backgrounds.
Additive	Why did Mrs. Fielding, a White woman, say to Ron nicely, "You can give me the books and I'll check them out for you"? In the book, what was the library's rule about Black people getting a library card?	What is the definition of *mission*? What does a librarian do and what is the purpose of a library? Why does Ron feel nervous and his hands get sweaty?	Draw a picture of a time you did something all by yourself and felt proud.	How did you feel doing something all by yourself? Do you think Ron made the right decision to tell Mrs. Fielding, "No, thanks, I'm going to do it all by myself"? What would you have said?	Do you consider Ron to be a hero? Survey your classmates and tally the votes. Interview the school librarian regarding the duties of a librarian.	How does Ron get the desk clerk in the library to respond to him? What would you have done? Use your imagination. Think outside the box.

Transformation	What do you think about the rule from a long time ago that only White people could check out books from the public library?	How do you think Black people felt about this rule? How would you feel if you were denied a library card?	Talk to your caregiver, mother, father, or a grandparent to see whether they ever had problems going to the library. Do they think the library's rule about checking out books back then was fair?	Do you agree with Ron's decision to jump on the counter of the library to get the desk clerk's attention? Would you have done the same thing or something different? Find out what is required to apply for a library card at your school and local libraries. What is the same and what is different about the application process?	Interview two or more friends or classmates and ask them what they would have done if the desk clerk in the library did not pay attention to them. What pattern do you see? Do you think calling the police for a little boy who was only 9 years old was the right thing to do to solve the problem? Explain. Do you think calling Ron's mother was a good idea? Explain.
					Create a rule that allows all people, regardless of race, to check out books.
Social Action	Why can't Ron check out books from the library like everyone else? List the reasons and come up with one or more recommendations to challenge this policy.	Talk to a friend or classmate about how you think Ron must have felt when he received his first library card.	Make a list of rules that you believe are unfair regarding library policies. Share with the librarian.	If you were the head librarian, what would you do to help children and adults sign up for a card? Share a few ideas.	Research stories about other Black boys who, like Ron, made a difference in their community by standing up for what was right.*
					Create and display posters of children from diverse backgrounds, but especially Black boys, holding their public library card and/or a book. Post it in the school library.

Matrix design adapted from Ford (2011). The authors recommend that teachers be mindful of and sensitive to engaging students in discussions that focus on discrimination based on race set in a particular time period. It is important not to embarrass students, which would be culturally insensitive and assaultive. Equally important to help children understand that, as a society, we have much work to do with regard to race relations. Finally, we recommend that teachers read the work of York (2016).

*Share the following link with students about an 11-year-old Black boy who starts a club for young Black boys to see themselves in books: www.huffingtonpost.com/entry/book-club-for-black-boys_us_58c7f308e4b081a56def641d

CHAPTER 5

Classroom Strategies for Success with Black Boys

They (My White Teachers) . . .

My parents told me I was a gifted Black boy. They said my parents were wrong. They said gifted education is for more advanced students. They said test scores do not lie. They told me Columbus discovered America. My father told me civilizations were already here. They said my father was wrong. They told me that Black people were slaves. My pastor said they were kings and queens, great scientists, mathematicians, writers, musicians, and farmers. They said my pastor was wrong. When I challenged their opinion, they said I was "overly aggressive" and to stop asking questions. They said I was "below average" academically. My parents said I was smart and one day I would become a teacher. They (my White teachers) told me to stop using African American Vernacular English. They never stopped to think that they were wrong. (Wright, Ford, & Grantham, 2018, p. 350)

This testimonial illustrates the all-too-familiar dismissive and condescending dialogue encountered by Black children, boys in particular, from their White female teachers with regard to what they learn in their homes and communities. Uncritical, unreflective White female teachers like those described above communicate a clear and complete disregard for this Black child's identity, voice, and agency, informed by unchecked biases situated in Eurocentric and westernized ideology. The teachers' responses to the Black boy clearly reflect unexamined Whiteness invoked by White social and cultural perspectives in accordance with White norms, truths, expectations, and experiences (Warren, 2013).

Every attempt that the Black boy makes to achieve affirmation, to embrace an identity of strength according to a culture filled with dignitaries, scholars, and artists, as well as the Black boy's own aspirations to become a teacher, is rejected by this White teacher. By telling the child to stop asking questions and using African American vernacular, the White teacher robs the child of his autonomy to use his authentic voice and to act with agency to contemplate critical, higher-order thinking and reasoning.

As we have argued throughout this book for urgent change, scenarios like this must become obsolete and regarded by all educators as a tragic past history that must stop repeating itself. Only through mutual commitment and conviction will we finally move ahead toward ensuring that all children, and especially Black boys, have access to high-quality educational experiences, materials, and activities needed to dramatically improve learner (and life) outcomes.

Chapter 3 laid out the important groundwork and foundation for changing Black boys' predominantly deficit-laden early childhood educational experiences and subsequent deficit learning outcomes by first changing the culture of deficit to a culture of success based on strengths and assets. Research literature consistently has pointed away from classroom cultures (like Boot Camps and Factories) that are dominated by a Direct Instruction approach taught by largely uncritical, unreflective practitioners who direct all teaching, and dole out punishments or rewards for obedience and compliance. Instead, research points clearly in the direction of creating constructivist, culturally responsive democratic learning communities of empowerment to best ensure high-quality early childhood experiences and outcomes for Black boys. Unlike the racist White female teacher described above, we must prepare future educators, as discussed in Chapter 3, to serve within classroom community cultures as constructivist, culturally responsive mentors who possess the needed empathy that can heighten their own awareness, understanding, and appreciation for the social and cultural uniqueness of Black boys.

The purpose of this chapter is to examine and discuss evidence-based practices that hold the greatest promise in achieving high-quality learning opportunities and experiences for Black boys, with maximum learner (and life) outcomes. Chapter 4 focused on the use of children's literature to support and promote Black boys' development of pride, self-esteem, and agency; this chapter will highlight STEM (science, technology, engineering, and math) content, materials, and activities.

HIGH-QUALITY, EVIDENCE-BASED APPROACHES USED IN CONSTRUCTIVIST, CULTURALLY RESPONSIVE, DEMOCRATIC LEARNING COMMUNITIES

As noted and elaborated in Chapter 3, constructivist, democratic learning communities strive to maximize the social setting for collaborative, cooperative learning groups in order to fully capitalize on critical, higher-order thinking and learning outcomes (Counsell et al., 2015; Counsell, Escalada, et al., 2016; Counsell, Uhlenberg, & Zan, 2013; DeVries & Sales, 2011; DeVries & Zan, 2012; DeVries, Zan, Hildebrandt, Edmiaston, & Sales,

2002). A constructivist classroom, however, is not truly democratic unless it guarantees absolute and full membership to everyone, and no one—in particular Black boys—is marginalized, oppressed, or excluded from asserting their voice and agency within all community activities. After all, as Kliewer (1998) asserts, "One does not learn membership apart from being a member" (p. 317). This means that all identities are seen and valued; all voices are heard and understood; and all needs are empathized with and satisfied to the greatest extent possible.

Current research has demonstrated that preschoolers from low-income, historically marginalized groups, and in particular Latino and Black boys, demonstrate high levels of self-regulation and other social–emotional skills required for later academic success (Fantuzzo, Coolahan, Mendez, McDermott, & Sutton-Smith, 1998; Galindo & Fuller, 2010; Li-Grining, 2012). It is instructionally advantageous and developmentally beneficial to structure learning in social settings that actively encourage intellectual exchanges using turn taking, brainstorming, problem solving, decisionmaking, multiple-perspective taking, and negotiating skills and processes (Boykin & Noguera, 2011; Johnson & Johnson, 2009).

A notable declaration by the Children's Defense Fund (2007) insists that "access to high-quality early education, especially for low-income students, can be the difference between a pathway that leads to the White House and one that leads to the jailhouse" (as cited in Johns, 2013, p. 55). Utilizing the constructivist approach to actively promote higher order, critical thinking and reasoning skills is a dramatic and deliberate departure from the superficial, surface-level, rote memorization of isolated facts and skills that is the primary focus of the Direct Instruction approach.

With this in mind, it is now important to consider which approaches best promote developmentally appropriate practices in ways that will be most beneficial and advantageous to Black boys. We examine three approaches that can greatly enhance the quality of Black boys' early childhood experiences: (1) the project approach, (2) project-based learning, and (3) problem-based learning.

The Project Approach

The project approach is not new, having origins that can be traced back to Dewey and the Progressive education movement, and is considered a centerpiece in the Bank Street approach. One hundred years ago, Kilpatrick (1918) described the "project method" as a curriculum based on "wholehearted purposeful activity proceeding in a social environment . . . the essential factor [being] the presence of a dominating purpose" (as cited in Kohn, 1999). The project approach has long since gained further attention and momentum because of its implementation in early childhood Reggio Emilia programs (Gandini, 1997; Helm & Beneke, 2003; Helm & Katz,

2011; Lewin-Benham, 2011; Wurm, 2005). Perhaps one of the best known and most widely recognized education researchers who has investigated and written extensively about the project approach is Lilian Katz (Helm & Katz, 2011; Katz & Chard, 2000).

The project approach encourages children to contemplate and propose projects (and subsequent goals) based on topics or subjects of interest to one or more children, often working cooperatively in small or large groups. There is evidence that many children enjoy self-directed, physically active learning in social groups, and Black boys are no exception. The diverse learning styles of Black boys and the project approach are compatible and complementary.

Brain research further supports the importance of movement in learning (Ratey, 2002). Because children's movement activates thinking, the more we encourage children to move during projects, the more we support and promote young children's ability to think, learn, and remember. In fact, Black boys especially thrive in social settings that allow them to actively explore and investigate in great depth any topic of interest that is compelling for them and therefore worth pursuing.

With these learning style claims in mind, we caution against the practice of essentializing Black boys or their experiences. By this we mean attributing "natural" and/or "essential characteristics" that suggests that Black boys display and/or engage in particular practices because of their race, group affiliation, or gender. Because there is enormous diversity within different racial, ethnic, and language groups, the experiences across and between individual and groups of Black boys should not be (mis)interpreted as static; rather, they are dynamic.

Like Gutiérrez and Rogoff (2003), who have warned against a simple "matching strategy," we similarly caution against this tendency to map certain cultural practices onto certain racial groups, or the "one style per person" mode of thinking. Both ways of thinking assume that an individual student's membership in a racial-ethnic group automatically tells teachers about this student's "style of learning." Overgeneralization can lead to stereotyping of Black boys and their perceived differences, and can result in a kind of cultural tracking (e.g., the acceptance of racial classification) whereby teachers plan curriculum and instruction and delivery of instruction based in large part on group categorization. Such practices, unfortunately, do not help early childhood teachers develop a nuanced understanding of the history of Black boys and their participation in diverse cultural communities; nor does the belief that "all Black children" learn this way account for within-group variation or change (Banks & Banks, 2010; Gutiérrez & Rogoff, 2003; Lee, 2007).

Continuing with the project approach, Katz and Chard (2000) assert that this approach is not intended to serve as a curriculum but rather as a way or means for actively engaging children's understanding, thinking, and reasoning. Unlike the scripted Direct Instruction curriculum with skill-drill activities and worksheets, the project approach is emergent in the sense that projects develop, evolve, and emerge in response to children's interests as well as compelling questions they encounter and unforeseen problems they feel compelled to pursue (Wien, 2008). The more opportunity Black boys have to engage in higher-order thinking, the more likely they will become confident problem-solvers and producers of culture and knowledge (Dodd-Nufrio, 2011; Ford, 2013). As observed by Kamii (1980), "Children who are confident in their ability to figure things out construct knowledge faster than those who do not have this confidence" (p. 13).

While questions often occur to children, teachers also can pose questions to help guide and facilitate Black boys' thinking and reasoning as they complete project work. As fellow travelers in constructivist, culturally responsive, democratic classroom communities, "ideas for projects originate in the continuum of the experience of children and teachers" (Hendrick, 2004, p. 23). Projects based on or connected to Black boys' lived experiences can include their diverse traditions, beliefs, and artifacts that are culturally meaningful and relevant, and thus are culturally responsive. Black boys' strong social and social–cognitive skills utilized to sustain peer-play interactions (Fantuzzo et al., 1998) can further enable them to successfully participate in extensive, complex projects as they develop and construct their own identity as learners and learn to understand and appreciate others' identities in comparison to their own as well.

In addition to supporting and guiding children's projects, early childhood educators teach themes (broad concepts and topics) and units (planned thematic lessons and activities) aligned with state and national standards (like the African American children's literature and activities described in Chapter 4). Learning and developmental centers within thoughtful, intentional democratic learning environments provide children in general—and Black boys in particular—with important opportunities to learn concepts and practice skills across content areas and developmental domains. It is, therefore, critical for educators working with young Black boys to strike a "balance" across teaching practices, strategies, and approaches.

As cautioned by Helm and Katz (2011), educators need to avoid and eliminate as much as possible mindless activities that largely fail to promote academic or intellectual goals. Tasks like coloring sheets offer little academic or developmental value and too often are justified as fun or entertaining. As noted in Chapters 3 and 4, like all other children, Black boys prosper from stimulating, hands-on experiences that engage higher-order thinking and learning (Murphy & Nesby, 2002; Watkins, 2002). Tasks that minimize rather than accentuate the intellectual gifts and talents of Black boys can quickly bore and disengage young Black boys and lead to assumptions of off-task behavior that can then be reinterpreted and reinscribed as misbehavior by uncritical, unreflective practitioners.

Figure 5.1. Project Approach Three-Phase Process

Beginning	Investigation	Culmination
Teacher observes children to determine interests and help identify project topic for investigation.	Children explore and investigate the chosen topic.	Children complete a culminating event designed to capture and share their new knowledge and insights with others.

Source: Helm & Katz, 2011.

Planning and Implementation. According to Helm (2004), the project approach generally follows a three-phase process: beginning, investigation, and culmination (see Figure 5.1).

In the beginning phase of the project, the constructivist mentor carefully observes children during indoor and outdoor play, as well as during center time, in an intentional environment with a variety of activities and materials (e.g., an assortment of picture books and videos) for children to examine and explore (see Photo 5.1).

The teacher documents (using photos and anecdotal notes) chosen activities and asks questions to help narrow multiple topics for selection. As fellow travelers, teachers and children come together for class meeting as a

Photo 5.1. Children Look at Books on Different Topics

community to recite the day of the week, the month, and year (calendar), as well as to identify the letters and the color of the week (see Photo 5.2). Children also discuss; brainstorm; acknowledge a child or children who have been helpful, considerate, respectful, and/or changes to the classroom environment; and engage in problem solving. The dry erase board and other visual aids and graphics, such as semantic webs to help document and stimulate the conversation about a variety of topics and interests, are used.

In-depth investigations require an allotment of time that can cover a span of several days, weeks, or months. Materials and needed artifacts are based largely on the theme, topic, or concept that is under investigation.

In the second, investigation phase of a project, children explore and investigate their selected topic or idea of interest. This investigation includes a variety of activities such as fieldtrips and access to resources like visiting experts and artifacts. Families in general, and families of Black boys in particular, can play a key role as fellow travelers during this investigation phase. Families can help with fieldtrips, share their expertise, and discuss important cultural artifacts (Capezzuto & Da Ros-Voseles, 2001; Harte, 2010). As children learn new information about their selected topic, they complete a variety of activities such as developing written plans and constructing models, and also can perform artistic works such as songs and dramatic plays.

Photo 5.2. Class Meeting Used to Introduce Calendar, Letters, and Color of the Week, and Topic of Discussion (The Amazing Brain)

Photo courtesy of Porter-Leath

In the culminating phase of a project, the teacher assists children with the completion of a culminating event designed to capture and share their new knowledge and insights with others. A culminating event might be a song, poem, dramatic play, poster display, model, book, and so on.

Firebird Ballet Project. In-depth projects can easily be aligned with Common Core State Standards (CCSS). For example, Counsell, King, and Wright (2013) documented a project titled "Firebird Ballet Project" completed by a group of 3-year-olds in a university campus early childhood class. Children liked to role-play in the dramatic play center, pretending to be ballerinas. During the initial phase, the teacher used a dry erase board to create a semantic web of the children's ideas. One group of children indicated that they were interested in learning more about ballerinas.

During the investigation phase of the Firebird Ballet Project, children examined and talked about (CCSS–Speaking and Listening) ballet artifacts (e.g., ballet slippers, leotards, and tights) (CCSS–Language), read books, and looked at photos of actual ballets. For their project, they dictated their own story of a ballet, the "Firebird Ballet," to their teacher, largely inspired by a ballet photo. The children then created their own costumes for their live ballet performance.

The culminating event for the "Firebird Ballet" was this group's ballet performance for their classmates. The group book was then assembled with stick puppets as a take-home activity bag to check out and share with family members (see Photo 5.3). Complementary to this project and to challenge gender stereotypes, we recommend an investigation into the history of men and Black men in dance/ballet—for example, exposing Black boys to Alvin Ailey, an African American choreographer and activist who founded the Alvin Ailey American Dance Theater (www.alvinailey.org/about/alvin-ailey-american-dance-theater). Teachers can introduce Black boys to modern dance made popular by Alvin Ailey and explore the influence of modern dance on contemporary dance. Finally, teachers can plan a fieldtrip to a local dance theater or have dancers visit their classroom with the intent of conveying the message that dance is for everyone, across race, gender, and socioeconomic strata.

Wheels in Motion Project. This project is based on a physical science workshop at a local children's museum (Counsell, Peat, et al., 2015, 2016). During the initial phase, a teacher might observe a group of kindergarten Black boys (or girls) playing extensively with wheeled objects in the block area. The teacher observes the children racing cars, pushing cars along roadways made of blocks, and parking them within block structures. During a class meeting, the teacher could ask the boys and girls about what they like about the cars (CCSS–Speaking and Listening). Why do they like playing

Photo 5.3. Take-Home Activity Bag: "Firebird Ballet" Book and Stick Puppets

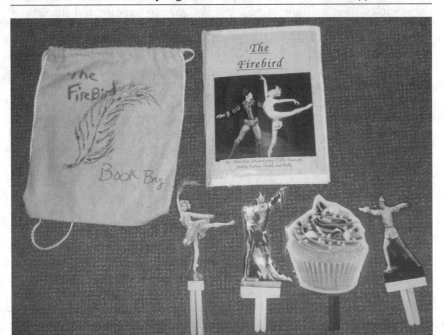

with the cars? How do the cars move? The children might decide they want to learn about wheels and how they work.

During the investigation phase of the Wheels in Motion Project, children can see how many different wheels are in the classroom (e.g., carts with wheels, office chair with wheels, toy cars, toy shopping cart, etc.) and observe how wheels are made with different materials, are of different sizes, and serve different purposes (CCSS–Language). The same group of children could bring different items with wheels from home to share and discuss (e.g., shoes with wheels, suitcases with wheels, skateboards, scooters, etc.).

The children could look at ground transportation books with different kinds of automobiles and other vehicles. They could digitally photograph or draw pictures and dictate stories about their illustrated cars.

The teacher could help the boys and girls to think about the "shape" of wheels and the relationship between shape and motion (i.e., circular shapes roll). The teacher could then challenge the children to make wheels of different shapes (squares, triangles, and hexagons) in the art center, using cardboard, to see how they move (CCSS–Geometry). For their project, the boys and girls decide to make their own models of cars.

Finally, the culminating event for the Wheels in Motion Project could be a car race. The children could make predictions about which car they think will be the fastest or which car will roll the farthest distance. It is important to note here that boys and girls should be encouraged to engage in the Wheels in Motion Project. As with the Firebird Ballet Project, we do not subscribe to gender stereotypes regarding "boy things" and "girl things." Likewise, we reject essentializing the interests of boys and girls based on gender stereotypes.

Successful project implementation by constructivist mentors, and children's full and active participation in projects, rely heavily on inclusive, culturally responsive, democratic learning communities that strive for empowerment, as described in Chapter 3. All children, and in particular Black boys, must be guaranteed active and full agency throughout the beginning, investigation, and culmination phases of the project. Otherwise, the learning experience will not support and promote the development of a healthy self-identity as a "strong and capable" researcher (Martalock, 2012, p. 7), needed to maximize learning and developmental outcomes.

In the end, children's explorations and investigations during project work come full circle, and as culturally responsive strengths-based, asset-based practices, projects empower Black boys with a sense of accomplishment that contributes directly toward a healthy self-identity, voice, and agency. Black boys' increased confidence and recognition as valued, contributing community members (Rahman, Yasin, & Yassin, 2012) prepare them as competent learners in both the short and long term (Griebling, 2011).

Culturally Responsive Studies: Project-Based and Problem-Based Learning

Helm and Katz (2011) also recognize similar approaches to project work. Like the project approach, project-based learning and problem-based learning also can guide and engage young children in deep, extensive, and meaningful investigations. Project-based learning most often entails the completion of projects that target content areas specifically aligned with curriculum and standards. A unit of study would entail multiple options from which children, working in cooperative groups, choose projects to research and investigate.

Problem-based learning, like the project approach and project-based learning, also empowers learners to identify real-world problems and questions that are worthy of exploration and to propose possible solutions. Kohn (1999) asserts that any approach using projects, regardless of the version, "incorporates facts and skills in the service of doing something that is as real and practical as it is intellectual and scholarly" (p. 148).

Within culturally responsive literature, York (2016) recommends long-term studies and projects as effective approaches to organizing, teaching, and learning at the early childhood level. Project-based learning units that focus on culturally relevant and anti-bias curriculum also are selected according to topics teachers consider important for children to learn as well as topics or questions that children find interesting. York provides a list of 25 common early childhood topics (see Figure 5.2) that can easily be expanded to include culturally relevant anti-bias values and related multicultural concepts.

Within the context of culture itself, Derman-Sparks and Edwards (2010) list important elements of "deep" culture (see Figure 5.3) that likewise can serve as broad topics for project-based learning.

Diverse, democratic learning communities provide unique opportunities filled with rich experiences to explore divergent beliefs, values, customs, and traditions across and within different groups of children, including Black boys. Rich conversations about cultural differences provide an important context for problem-based learning projects that not only promote children's development as researchers but expand their higher-order, critical thinking into the social sphere as activists for social change.

Much like the African American children's literature discussed in Chapter 4, there are a multitude of topics, concepts, and issues that may be encountered and need to be broached when diverse groups of children think, learn, grow, and work together. York (2016) proposes several activities that can easily be expanded into problem-based learning projects (see Figure 5.4).

Figure 5.2. Culturally Relevant Project-Based Learning Topics

Who Am I?	Clothes We Wear	Weather
Books	Food We Eat	Folktales
Boys and Girls	Alike and Different	Animals
Places People Live	Day and Night	Dance and Movement
Friends	Light and Dark	Pets
Toys and Games	Feelings	Bodies
Families	Five Senses	Colors
Transportation	Heroes and Sheroes	
Our Community	Music	

Source: York, 2016, p. 224. Reprinted with permission of Redleaf Press.

Figure 5.3. Deep Culture Project-Based Learning Topics

Languages	Migration	Emotions
Values	Work	Recreation
Extended Family Members	Housing	Health Care

Source: Derman-Sparks & Edwards, 2010, p. 56. Reprinted with permission of NAEYC.

Figure 5.4. Culturally Relevant Problem-Based Learning Topics (Promoting Activism)

Superheroes		
Cooperation	Martin's Dream (Social Responsibility)	Don't Leave Us Out
Work It Out	Walk Away	Human Rights
Kindness Pledge	Tributes	Bias-Free Zone
Stand Up	No Name-Calling	Group Think
Courage	Stand by Me	Classroom Rights
Think and Act for Yourself	Thanks and No Thanks	Speak Up

Source: York, 2016, pp. 294–311. Reprinted with permission of Redleaf Press.

While the project approach, project-based learning, and problem-based learning can easily integrate concepts and skills across academic content and developmental domains, as described and illustrated throughout this chapter, there is perhaps one content area in particular that lends itself to active investigation—science. Young children are surrounded by nature, and thus Black boys can make important real-world connections and construct mental relationships that help them make sense of their world and the role they play in it, inside and outside of school. However, young children in early childhood education have very limited, if any, formal opportunities to explore and investigate physical science concepts and relationships. Providing young children, Black boys in particular, with high-quality experiences in physical science is important and provides a firm foundation for later STEM learning that can lead to eventual STEM careers.

Ramps and Pathways Promotes Active Inquiry and Investigation. Ramps and Pathways (R&P) has arguably emerged as one of the most promising STEM activities and materials designed to improve early childhood educators' STEM teaching practices and increase young children's STEM outcomes (Counsell, 2011, 2017b; Counsell, Escalada, et al., 2016; Counsell, Uhlenberg, & Zan, 2013; DeVries & Sales, 2011). R&P was developed at a constructivist laboratory demonstration school, the Freeburg School, serving students from a low-income neighborhood in Waterloo, Iowa, in which it was located. Between 85% and 92% of the children at Freeburg qualified for free or reduced lunch, and more than 70% were African American (DeVries & Sales, 2011).

R&P programs consist of young children (ages 3–8) building ramp structures and pathways with lengths of cove molding, and then releasing marbles on their structures (exploration and investigation) and observing what happens (see Photo 5.4).

Photo 5.4. A Child Observes, Explores, and Investigates with R&P

R&P materials and activities easily allow for an adapted three-phase, learning-cycle approach that encourages exploration, concept development, and application as children investigate with ramps (Cooney, Escalada, & Unruh, 2008). During R&P investigations, young children actively experience and develop practical understanding of Newton's laws of force and motion in relation to inclines (Counsell, 2017b; Counsell, Escalada, et al., 2016; Counsell, Uhlenberg, & Zan, 2013; Counsell & Wright, 2016; DeVries & Sales, 2011; Zan & Geiken, 2010).

R&P encourages all children to construct STEM knowledge, understanding, and relationships as they actively engage with R&P materials and share and interpret what they experience in social settings. As in project-based and problem-based learning, during R&P investigations children are encouraged to pursue agendas that interest them, seek to answer compelling questions (e.g., How do I make the marble jump?), and figure out problems they encounter (e.g., Why didn't the marble turn the corner?) (see Photo 5.5).

As children explore and investigate in pairs, small groups, and large groups, they learn to collaborate and cooperate by negotiating, taking multiple perspectives, brainstorming, and problem solving together. Because children in general, and Black boys in particular, have preferences for hands-on experiences using multisensory materials, R&P can be an appealing set of materials and activities that allow Black boys to thrive during investigations (see Photo 5.6).

Photo 5.5. A Child Pursues Compelling Questions Using R&P

Photo 5.6. Children Complete Investigations in Cooperative Groups

R&P creates authentic contexts that are intrinsically motivating for children to communicate their thoughts as well as listen to the thoughts of others, aligned with the CCSS. Language and communication skills are promoted as children take turns to both ask one another questions and answer them (CCSS–Speaking and Listening), share ideas, make observations, and offer suggestions (Van Meeteren, 2016). Rich conversations during meaningful, relevant investigations help children expand their oral language using new words and vocabulary (CCSS–Language) to describe the different materials they use and how objects move differently (Counsell & Sander, 2016). Children who are intrinsically interested in what they are doing are also self-motivated to communicate with others, documenting their experience by drawing illustrations of their ramp structures with written descriptions and explanations (see Photo 5.7).

As Black boys investigate with R&P, they are exposed to and use a wide assortment of logical–mathematical skills and concepts aligned with CCSS–Mathematics. For example, children use spatial awareness as they figure out where and how to place each ramp in their structure. Ramp sections have different lengths (ramps are cut in 1-, 2-, 3-, and 4-foot lengths) that children can combine and add to other section lengths (CCSS–Operations and Algebraic Thinking) to measure the entire length of each ramp trajectory

Photo 5.7. A Child Draws and Writes About Ramps

(CCSS–Measurement and Data). Black boys can count how many blocks they stack (CCSS–Counting and Cardinality) to support ramps and measure the height at the top of the ramp (CCSS–Measurement and Data). Different blocks have different geometric shapes (CCSS–Geometry) and solids (triangles, circles, squares, spheres, cubes, cones, and cylinders). Children can group, sort, and classify shapes to be used in ramp structures in different ways for different purposes. Children, in general, frequently create geometric patterns, order, seriation, and symmetry with their ramp structures (see Photo 5.8).

Children can release different marbles of different sizes, weight, mass, and circumferences. During R&P investigations, Black boys use scientific thinking to create or invent something with an intended purpose. Basic engineering design process entails children asking what they want to construct, imagining it, planning how to construct it, creating it, and improving upon their structure (Cunningham, 2009), a process that has clear appeal to some Black boys. As they use basic engineering design during R&P, they ask themselves what they want the marble to do; imagine and plan how to position ramps; create a ramp structure; and improve upon their structure to best achieve the desired outcome (e.g., make the marble jump, fly, turn a corner, speed up, or slow down).

Photo 5.8. A Child Constructs a Ramp Structure with a Pattern

Technology encompasses the devices, capabilities, and knowledge used to satisfy or address wants or needs. R&P provides children with real-world technology applications as they build and investigate ramp structures. As Black boys design increasingly complex structures, they explore a variety of materials (e.g., plastic tubing, hot wheel tracks, cardboard boxes) to create new ramp technology like loops, tunnels, and supports (see Photo 5.9).

R&P materials and activities provide Black boys and teachers with opportunities for language-rich STEM conversations around logical–mathematical concepts and skills, and about how to design and use technology, during the basic engineering design process. R&P cannot guarantee that all children will achieve the same STEM outcomes. As discussed in Chapter 3, children's gifts, talents, skills, and abilities are largely unknown, especially if we do not give them an opportunity to demonstrate what they know and understand about a variety of different topics, which is often the case with Black boys. Therefore, it is imperative to maximize learning opportunities and experiences in order to maximize every child's (and certainly every Black boy's) learning and developmental outcomes. Creating high-quality learning experiences like R&P that are educationally relevant and personally respectful to all children, and in particular Black boys, empowers them with a self-identity, voice, and agency as confident and capable STEM learners and investigators.

Photo 5.9. Children Apply Basic Engineering Design to Use and Create Technology

CONCLUSION

In Alfie Kohn's (1999) book *The Schools Our Children Deserve: Moving Beyond Traditional Classrooms and Tougher Standards*, he declared that the "one place where traditional teaching rules with a vengeance is in urban or inner-city schools, which are generally euphemisms for those attended by children of color from low-income families" (p. 9). In these schools where teacher expectations are low, there is often a focus on remedial and basic skills development. According to Kohn, as long as key stakeholders and decisionmakers continue to embrace the assumption that traditional, back-to-the-basics, skill-drill, direct instructional approaches and strategies are the best approach with Black children, "alternative ways of teaching will rarely be used even if the evidence supports their value for all children" (p. 11), as we likewise have argued throughout this book.

Kohn largely credits Lilian Katz and Sylvia Chard for having "revolutionized preschool education" with engaging, higher-order critical thinking opportunities and experiences using the project approach. We now ask, When will Black boys be guaranteed full access to revolutionized preschool experiences using high-quality teaching strategies and approaches—like the project approach and STEM investigations (such as Ramps and Pathways)? When will we see as many "mirror" books representing Black boys' culture as we see "window" books representing White children's culture in every early childhood classroom?

This book is an urgent and resounding call to action. We set out to review the statistical data regarding (1) preschool suspension and expulsion rates, (2) later academic achievement gaps, (3) overrepresentation in special education, and (4) eventual (preschool-to-prison) incarceration rates. Our reason for providing these data was to demonstrate the current status of Black boys in the United States, past and present. We have examined the research and used learning and developmental theory to guide and inform which teaching styles, approaches, strategies, materials, and classroom cultures hold the greatest promise for maximizing Black boys' learning and development—and which ones to avoid and eliminate at all costs. We also challenge the practice of essentializing Black boys and their experiences based on their racial-ethnic affiliations. We must now unite in solidarity not only as fellow travelers with Black boys, their families, and communities, but also as fellow advocates who are committed to change—guaranteeing high-quality early childhood experiences for everyone, and especially the brilliance of Black boys.

Resources for Building Cultural Competence in Early Childhood Teachers

Despite efforts in teacher preparation programs to prepare highly qualified (i.e., steeped in content with sophisticated pedagogical practices) teachers and teacher candidates to work effectively with "other people's children," the anecdotal and empirical evidence we have shared throughout this book demonstrates that we still have a long way to go in seeing differences among students as assets rather than deficits. Time and again, the authors hear from principals that they continue to hire new teachers who, despite what they shared during their interviews, are not culturally competent. These principals lament about the amount of resources and time required to provide additional teacher preparation in the way of professional development. In meetings with principals, we are invariably asked the question, "What are you all doing over there in higher education?"

Their question almost always leaves us wondering how we can do a better job of preparing preservice teachers to work effectively with children and their families from culturally, linguistically, and economically diverse backgrounds. Although the synergy across our different areas of expertise, disciplinary perspectives, research interests, theoretical stances, and personal and professional experiences fuels our resolve to continue to challenge teacher candidates as we do ourselves, we know that to prepare highly qualified teachers, early childhood teacher education requires a combination of the following:

1. rigorous coursework involving exposure to critical readings and promising practices in the field
2. activities that challenge teacher candidates' attitudes, beliefs, and practices
3. first-rate field experiences (student teaching/residency) that expose teacher candidates to diverse perspectives/multiple points of view
4. mentor teachers who themselves are culturally steeped in content knowledge, possess sophisticated pedagogical practices, and are culturally competent

5. dedicated professors committed to cultural competence, willing to challenge resistant teacher education candidates who hold colorblind ideologies and stereotypes that blind them from seeing promise in all students of color, especially Black boys

As discussed in Chapter 4, self-reflection is essential to interrogating attitudes, beliefs, and practices to determine how these ways of knowing and being shape and inform how teachers engage with and respond to children and families who look like them and those who do not. This is a career-long process. There is never a point when one "arrives"; rather, this work is lifelong and not limited to schools and classrooms, but must be applied in one's daily life. Children are perceptive; they will know if one's "anti-bias," "multicultural" persona is genuine beyond the school day.

We find, albeit to varying degrees, from our own racial backgrounds (first author, Black male; second author, White female) that many of our students (mostly White females) have grown up in environments where they lay claims to having been exposed to racial, linguistic, and economic diversity, and believe these personal experiences alone make them culturally competent. In general, we encounter teacher candidates who believe they already have the requisite knowledge, skills, and dispositions to work with other people's children. It is not long after such claims have been made that resistance to controversial content manifests. Despite the reality of now having diverse peer groups, many have not been required to take a critical look at the world or their position in it.

For this and other critical reasons, we conclude this book with a resources section aimed solely at supporting teacher educators in their work to prepare teachers who are steeped in content knowledge and culturally competent. We have found that this requires debunking the myths that early childhood education, as a major, is "easy" and "fun." Yes, learning should be fun, but fun is a byproduct of the critical importance of teaching and learning that cares for the whole child. It is our hope that the resources included here will go a long way in supporting the preparation of highly qualified early childhood professionals who will see and promote the strengths of all children, Black boys especially. All children deserve high-quality teachers; all children deserve culturally competent teachers.

ACADEMIC/PROFESSIONAL JOURNALS

Child Development, onlinelibrary.wiley.com/journal/10.1111/(ISSN)1467-8624

Diverse Issues in Higher Education, diverseeducation.com

Early Childhood Development and Care, www.tandfonline.com/loi/gecd20

Early Childhood Education Journal, link.springer.com/journal/10643
Early Childhood Research & Practice, ecrp.uiuc.edu/
Early Childhood Research Quarterly, www.journals.elsevier.com/early-childhood-research-quarterly/
Early Childhood Today, teacher.scholastic.com/products/ect/
Early Years: Journal of International Research and Development, www.ingentaconnect.com/content/routledg/ceye
Education and Urban Society, eus.sagepub.com
Gifted Child Today, journals.sagepub.com/home/gct
Journal of African American Males in Education, journalofafricanamericanmales.com/; "K–16 and Beyond: African American Male Student Engagement in STEM Disciplines" [Special issue on STEM education], 2(1), Guest editor Dr. Brian L. Wright, journalofafricanamericanmales.com/vol2no1/
Journal of Negro Education, www.journalnegroed.org
Multiple Voices for Ethnically Diverse Exceptional Learners, community.cec.sped.org/ddel/publications
Teaching Young Children, www.naeyc.org/publications
Urban Education, uex.sagepub.com
Urban Review, link.springer.com/journal/11256
Young Children, www.naeyc.org/publications

AUTHENTIC MULTICULTURAL CHILDREN'S BOOKS WITH BLACK BOYS AS PROTAGONISTS

Abdul-Jabbar, K., Raymond Obstfeld, B. B. (Illus.), & Ford, A.G. (Illus.). (2012). *What color is my world? The lost history of African-American inventors*. Somerville, MA: Candlewick Press.

Alalou, E., & Essakalli, J. K. (Illus.). (2008). *The butter man*. Watertown, MA: Charlesbridge.

Barasch, L. (2004). *Knockin' on wood starring Peg Leg Bates*. New York, NY: Lee & Low Books.

Blue, R., Naden, C. J., & Tate, D. (Illus.). (2009). *Ron's big mission*. New York, NY: Dutton Children's Books/Penguin Group.

Bolden, T., & Christie, R. G. (Illus.). (2004). *The champ: The story of Muhammad Ali*. New York, NY: Knopf.

Bradby, M., & Soentpiet, C. (Illus.). (1995). *More than anything else*. New York, NY: Orchard Books.

Burleigh, R., & Los, M. (Illus.). (2001). *Lookin' for bird in the big city*. San Diego, CA: Harcourt.

Clifton, L., & Grifalconi, A. (Illus.). (1988). *Everett Anderson's goodbye*. New York, NY: Holt.

Cline-Ransome, L., & Ransome, J. (Illus.). (2000). *Satchel Paige*. New York, NY: Simon & Schuster.

Cline-Ransome, L., & Ransome, J. (Illus.). (2004). *Major Taylor: Champion cyclist.* New York, NY: Atheneum.

Cline-Ransome, L., & Ransome, J. (Illus.). (2007). *Young Pelé: Soccer's first star.* New York, NY: Atheneum.

Collier, B. (2000). *Uptown.* New York, NY: Holt.

Cooper, F. (1994). *Coming home: From the life of Langston Hughes.* New York, NY: Putnam.

Cooper, F. (1996). *Mandela: From the life of the South African statesman.* New York, NY: Philomel.

Cooper, M., & Bennett, N. (2000). *Gettin' through Thursday.* New York, NY: Lee & Low Books.

Crowe, C. (2012). *Just as good: How Larry Doby changed America's game.* Somerville, MA: Candlewick Press.

Curtis, G., & Lewis, E. B. (Illus.). (1998). *The bat boy and his violin.* New York, NY: Simon & Schuster.

Danticat, E., & Delinois, A. (Illus.). (2010). *Eight days: A story of Haiti.* New York, NY: Orchard Books.

Diggs, T., & Evans, S. W. (Illus.). (2011). *Chocolate me!* New York, NY: Square Fish/Feiwel Friends/Imprints of Macmillan.

Drummond, J. B., Bynum, B. K., & McGee, B. (Illus.). (2016). *I'm a brilliant little Black boy!* Los Angeles, CA: DreamTitle.

Duggleby, J., & Lawrence, J. (Illus.). (1998). *Story painter: The life of Jacob Lawrence.* San Francisco, CA: Chronicle Books.

Elvgren, J. R. (2006). *Josias, hold the book.* Honesdale, PA: Boyds Mills Press.

Evans, S. W. (2009). *Olu's dream.* New York, NY: Katherine Tegen Books.

Farris, C. K., & Soentpiet, C. (Illus.). (2003). *My brother Martin: A sister remembers growing up with the Rev. Dr. Martin Luther King, Jr.* New York, NY: Simon & Schuster.

Greenfield, E., & Ford, G. (Illus.). (2009). *Paul Robeson.* New York, NY: Lee & Low Books. (Original work published 1975)

Grimes, N., & Benny, M. (Illus.). (2008). *Oh, brother!* New York, NY: HarperCollins/Amistad.

Grimes, N., & Collier, B. (Illus.). (2008). *Barack Obama: Son of promise, child of hope.* New York, NY: Simon & Schuster.

Halfmann, J., & Smith, D. (Illus.). (2008). *Seven miles to freedom: The Robert Smalls story.* New York, NY: Lee & Low Books.

Haskins, J., Benson, K., & Andrews, B. (Illus.). (2006). *John Lewis in the lead: A story of the Civil Rights Movement.* New York, NY: Lee & Low Books.

Hoffman, M., & Littlewood, K. (Illus.). (2002). *The colour of home.* London, England: Frances Lincoln.

Hubbard, C., & Belford, K. (Illus.). (2010). *Game set match champion: Arthur Ashe.* New York, NY: Lee & Low Books.

Hubbard, C., & McGuire, R. (Illus.). (2008). *The last Black king of the Kentucky derby.* New York, NY: Lee & Low Books.

Hudson, W., & Ambush, P. (Illus.). (2008). *It's church going time.* New York, NY: Marimba Books.

Hudson, W., & Ford, G. (Illus.). (1991). *Jamal's busy day.* Orange, NJ: Just Us Books.

Igus, T., & Bond, H. (Illus.). (1992). *When I was little*. Orange, NJ: Just Us Books.

Issa, K. J., & Dawson, A. L. (2008). *Howard Thurman's great hope*. New York, NY: Lee & Low Books.

Johnson, A. (1997). *Daddy calls me a man*. New York, NY: Orchard Books.

Johnson, G. F., & Tokumbo, D. (Illus.). (2004). *Has anybody lost a glove?* Honesdale, PA: Boyds Mills Press.

Jordan, B., Wright, C. V., & Hu, Y. H. (Illus.). (2006). *I told you I can play!* East Orange, NJ: Just Us Books.

Jordan, R., Jordan, D., & Nelson, K. (Illus.). (2000). *Salt in his shoes: Michael Jordan in pursuit of a dream*. New York, NY: Simon & Schuster.

Kessler, C., & Jenkins, L. (Illus.). (2006). *Best beekeeper of Lalibela*. New York, NY: Holiday House.

Lauture, D., & Green, J. (Illus.). (1992). *Father and son*. New York, NY: Philomel.

Lessac, F. (1984). *My little island*. New York, NY: HarperCollins.

MacLeod, E. (2007). *George Washington Carver: An innovative life*. Tonawanda, NY: Kids Can.

Mathis, S. B., & Ford, G. (Illus.). (2001). *Ray Charles*. New York, NY: Lee & Low Books. (Original work published 1973)

McDonough, Y. Z., & Zeldis, M. (Illus.). (2002). *Peaceful protest: The life of Nelson Mandela*. New York, NY: Walker.

Medina, T., & Watson, J. J. (Illus.). (2009). *I and I*. New York, NY: Lee & Low Books.

Miller, W., & Christie, R. G. (Illus.). (1997). *Richard Wright and the library card*. New York, NY: Lee & Low Books.

Miller, W., & Pate, R. S. (Illus.). (2004). *Joe Louis, my champion*. New York, NY: Lee & Low Books.

Mollel, T., & Lewis, E. B. (Illus.). (1999). *My rows and piles of coins*. New York, NY: Clarion Books.

Myers, W. D., & Jenkins, L. (Illus.). (2000). *Malcolm X: A fire burning brightly*. New York, NY: HarperCollins.

Nolen, J., & Nelson, K. (Illus.). (2005). *Hewitt Anderson's great big life*. New York, NY: Simon & Schuster.

Parker, R. A. (2008). *Piano starts here: The young Art Tatum*. New York, NY: Schwartz & Wade.

Pinkney, A. D., & Pinkney, B. (Illus.). (1998). *Duke Ellington: The piano prince and his orchestra*. New York, NY: Hyperion.

Pinkney, B. (1994). *Max found two sticks*. New York, NY: Simon & Schuster.

Rappaport, D., & Collier, B. (Illus.). (2001). *Martin's big words: The life of Dr. Martin Luther King, Jr.* New York, NY: Hyperion.

Raschka, C. (1992). *Charlie Parker played be bop*. New York, NY: Scholastic.

Raschka, C. (1993). *Yo! Yes!* New York, NY: Orchard Books.

Raven, M. T., & Ellison, C. (Illus.). (2005). *Let them play*. Chelsea, MI: Sleeping Bear Press.

Smalls-Hector, I., & Hays, M. (Illus.). (1992). *Jonathan and his mommy*. Boston, MA: Little, Brown.

Smith, C. R., & Collier, B. (Illus.). (2007). *Twelve rounds to glory: The story of Muhammad Ali*. Cambridge, MA: Candlewick Press.

Steptoe, J. (1969). *Stevie*. New York, NY: HarperCollins.

Steptoe, J. (2003). *The Jones family express*. New York, NY: Lee & Low Books.

Steptoe, J., & Lewis, E. B. (Illus.). (1997). *Creativity*. New York, NY: Clarion Books.

Stuve-Bodeen, S., & Boyd, A. (Illus.). (2003). *Babu's song*. New York, NY: Lee & Low Books.

Tarpley, N., & Lewis, E. B. (Illus.). (2003). *Bibbity bop barbershop*. Boston, MA: Little, Brown.

Tarpley, N., & Lewis, E. B. (Illus.). (2003). *Joe-Joe's first flight*. New York, NY: Knopf.

Tavares, M. (2012). *Henry Aaron's dream*. Somerville, MA: Candlewick Press.

Tate, D., & Christie, R. G. (Illus.). (2012). *It jes' happened: When Bill Traylor started to draw*. New York, NY: Lee & Low Books.

Taulbert, C. L., & Lewis, E. B. (Illus.). (2001). *Little Cliff's first day of school*. New York, NY: Dial.

Taylor, G., & Morrison, F. (Illus.). (2006). *George Crum and the Saratoga Chip*. New York, NY: Lee & Low Books.

Towle, W., & Clay, W. (Illus.). (1993). *The real McCoy: The life of an African-American inventor*. New York, NY: Scholastic.

Troupe, Q., & Cohen, L. (Illus.). (2005). *Little Stevie Wonder*. New York, NY: Houghton Mifflin.

Watts, J. H., & Marshall, F. (Illus.). (1997). *Keepers*. New York, NY: Lee & Low Books.

Weatherford, C. B., & Qualls, S. (Illus.). (2008). *Before John was a jazz giant: A song of John Coltrane*. New York, NY: Holt.

Weidhorn, M. (1993). *Jackie Robinson*. New York, NY: Atheneum.

Williams, M., & Christie, R. G. (Illus.). (2005). *Brothers in hope: The story of the lost boys of Sudan*. New York, NY: Lee & Low Books.

Youme. (2004). *Sélavi: A Haitian story of hope*. El Paso, TX: Cinco Puntos.

EARLY CHILDHOOD/CHILD DEVELOPMENT WEBSITES FOR TEACHERS

Association for Childhood Education International, Special Interest Forum—Educating Black Boys and Adolescent Males (EBBAM), www.acei.org/community/

Center on the Developing Child/Harvard University, developingchild.harvard.edu/

National Association for the Education of Young Children (NAEYC), www.naeyc.org/

National Black Child Development Institute, www.nbcdi.org/

Zero to Three, www.zerotothree.org/

PROFESSIONAL ASSOCIATIONS/ORGANIZATIONS
AND CONFERENCES AND SYMPOSIA

Alliance for Boys and Men of Color, www.facebook.com/
AllianceforBMOC/

American Educational Research Association (e.g., Un-AERA, Research
Focus on Black Education), www.aera.net/

Coalition of Schools Educating Boys of Color, www.coseboc.org/

Council for Exceptional Children, Division for Culturally and
Linguistically Diverse Exceptional Learners (CEC-DDEL), community.
cec.sped.org/ddel/home, and Division for Early Childhood (DEC),
www.dec-sped.org

Council of the Great City Schools, www.cgcs.org/

International Colloquium on Black Males in Education, globalcolloquium.
org/

National Alliance of Black School Educators, www.nabse.org/

National Association for Gifted Children, Special Populations network,
G-RACE Special Interest Group, and Early Childhood network, www.
nagc.org

National Association for Multicultural Education, nameorg.org/

National Black Male Retreat, odi.osu.edu/bell-national-resource-center/
events/african-american-male-retreat/

National Education Association, www.nea.org

National Head Start Association, www.nhsa.org/

Research Focus on Black Education SIG of AERA, www.aera.net/SIG085/
Research-Focus-on-Black-Education-SIG

RISE for Boys and Men of Color, www.risebmoc.org/pages/about

Society for Research in Child Development, www.srcd.org/

EDUCATION CENTERS AND INSTITUTES

African American Male Achievement/Oakland Unified School District,
www.ousd.org/Domain/78

Black Male Institute/UCLA, blackmaleinstitute.org/

Center for the Study of Race & Equity in Education, www.gse.upenn.edu/
equity/

Harlem Children's Zone, hcz.org/

Institute for Urban and Minority Education, iume.tc.columbia.edu/

Scholar Identity Institute, www.drdonnayford.com/services3

UCLA Center X, centerx.gseis.ucla.edu/

The Urban Child Institute, www.urbanchildinstitute.org/

RESEARCH REPORTS ON BLACK MALES

Black Lives Matter: The Schott 50 State Report on Public Education and Black Males, John H. Jackson, President and CEO, www.blackboysreport.org/2015-black-boys-report.pdf

Breaking Barriers 2: Plotting the Path to Academic Success for School-age African American Males, Ivory A. Toldson, www.cbcfinc.org/oUploadedFiles/BreakingBarriers2.pdf

The Condition of Education 2017, nces.ed.gov/pubs2017/2017144.pdf

The Counter Narrative: Reframing Success of High Achieving Black and Latino Males in Los Angeles County, Tyrone C. Howard & Associates, diversity.utexas.edu/projectmales/wp-content/uploads/2016/12/CounterNarrative-f-Dec16.pdf

Succeeding in the City: A Report from the New York City Black and Latino Male High School Achievement Study, Shaun Harper & Associates, www.gse.upenn.edu/equity/sites/gse.upenn.edu.equity/files/publications/Harper_and_Associates_2014.pdf

Teaching Young Men of Color: Teacher Voices, The National Writing Center, www.nwp.org/cs/public/download/nwp_file/18401/2013_Teacher_Voices_Report.pdf?x-r=pcfile_d

BLACK MALE TEACHER INITIATIVES

Black Men Teaching Initiative, blackmenteaching.org/index.php?option=com_content&view=article&id=1&itemid=102

The Boston Public Schools Male Educators of Color Executive Coaching Program (MEOC), www.teachboston.org/diversity-in-bps

Call Me MISTER, www.clemson.edu/education/callmemister/

The Honoré Center, generalhonore.com/the-honore-center/

NYC Men Teach, www1.nyc.gov/site/ymi/teach/nyc-men-teach.page

Teacher Quality & Retention Program (TQRP)/Thurgood Marshall College Fund, tmcf.org/our-programs/k-12-education/teacher-quality-retention-program

SPOTLIGHT ON A CURRENT BLACK MALE INITIATIVE: W.E.B. DUBOIS ACADEMY

W.E.B. DuBois Academy, schools.jefferson.kyschools.us/middle/DuBoisAcademy/#hero

This is a Jefferson County Public Schools middle school program that is expected to start with 150 6th-graders in the 2018–2019 school year and is budgeted to cost $5.8 million over its first 3 years. (See www.courier-journal.com/story/news/education/2017/06/28/jcps-board-gives-thumbs-up-males-color-academy/430573001/)

References

Adamu, M., & Hogan, L. (2015). *Point of entry: The preschool-to-prison pipeline.* Washington, DC: Center for American Progress.

Alexander, M. (2010). *The new Jim Crow: Mass incarceration in the age of color-blindness.* New York, NY: The New Press.

Allen, Q., & White-Smith, K. (2015). "Just as bad as prison": The challenge of dismantling the school-to-prison pipeline through teacher and community education. *Equity and Excellence, 47*(4), 445–460.

Allington, R., McGill-Franzen, A., Camilli, G., Williams, L., Graff, J., Zeig, J., & Nowak, R. (2010). Addressing summer setbacks among economically disadvantaged elementary students. *Reading Psychology, 31*, 411–427.

Anderson, E. (Ed.). (2008). *Against the wall: Poor, young, Black, and male.* Philadelphia: University of Pennsylvania Press.

Anderson, L. W. (Ed.), Krathwohl, D. R. (Ed.), Airasian, P. W., Cruikshank, K. A., Mayer, R. E., Pintrich, P. R., Raths, J., & Wittrock, M. C. (2004). *A taxonomy for learning, teaching, and assessing: A revision of Bloom's taxonomy of educational objectives* (Complete ed.). New York, NY: Longman.

Annie E. Casey Foundation. (2010). Early warning! Why reading by the end of third grade matters. Retrieved from www.aecf.org/resources/early-warning-why-reading-by-the-end-of-third-grade-matters/

Aud, S., Hussar, W., Kena, G., Bianco, K., Frohlich, L., Kemp, J., & Tahan, K. (2011). *The condition of education 2011* (NCES 2011-033). Washington, DC: U.S. Government Printing Office.

Ballenger, C. (1999). *Teaching other people's children: Literacy and learning in a bilingual classroom.* New York, NY: Teachers College Press.

Banks, J. A. (1994). *Multiethnic education: Theory and practice* (3rd ed.). Needham Heights, MA: Allyn & Bacon.

Banks, J. A. (2009). *Teaching strategies for ethnic studies* (8th ed.). New York, NY: Allyn & Bacon.

Banks, J. A. (2014). *An introduction to multicultural education* (5th ed.). Boston, MA: Pearson.

Banks, J. A., & Banks, C. A. M. (Eds.). (2010). *Multicultural education: Issues and perspectives* (7th ed.). Hoboken, NJ: Wiley.

Barbarin, O. A. (2013). A longitudinal examination of socioemotional learning in African American and Latino boys across the transition from pre-K to kindergarten, *American Journal of Orthopsychiatry, 83*(2–3), 156–164.

Barbarin, O. A., & Crawford, G. M. (2006). Acknowledging and reducing stigmatization of African American boys. *Young Children, 61*(6), 79–86.

Barbarin, O. A., Murry, V., Tolan, P., & Graham, S. (2016). Development of boys and young men of color: Implications of developmental science for my brother's keeper initiative. *Social Policy Report, 29*(3), 1–31.

Barnett, W. S., Carolan, M., & Johns, D. (2013). *Equity and excellence: African-American children's access to quality preschool.* New Brunswick, NJ: National Institute for Early Education Research. Retrieved from nieer.org/wp-content/uploads/2016/08/Equity20and20Excellence20African-American20ChildrenE28099s20Access20to20Quality20Preschool_0.pdf

Barnett, W. S., Epstein, D. J., Carolan, M. E., Ackerman, D. J., & Friedman, A. H. (2010). *The state of preschool 2010.* New Brunswick, NJ: National Institute for Early Education Research.

Barnett, W. S., Hustedt, J. T., Friedman, A. H., Stevenson Boyd, J., & Ainsworth, P. (2007) *The state of preschool 2007.* New Brunswick, NJ: National Institute for Early Education Research. Retrieved from http://nieer.org/wp-content/uploads/2016/10/2007yearbook.pdf

Bischoff, K., & Reardon, S. (2014). Residential segregation by income, 1970–2009. In J. Logan (Ed.), *Diversity and disparities: America enters a new century* (pp. 208–233). New York, NY: Russell Sage.

Bishop, R. S. (1990). Mirrors, windows, and sliding glass doors. In *Perspectives: Choosing and using books for the classroom, 6*(3), ix–xi.

Bishop, R. S. (1993). Multicultural literature for children: Making informed choices. In V. J. Harris (Ed.), *Teaching multicultural literature in grades K–8* (pp. 37–54). Norwood, MA: Christopher-Gordon.

Bishop, R. S. (2012). Reflections on the development of African American children's literature. *Journal of Children's Literature, 38*(2), 5–13.

Bloom, B. S. (Ed.). (1956). *Taxonomy of educational objectives: The classification of educational goals.* New York, NY: Longman.

Blue, R., & Naden, C. J. (2009). *Ron's big mission.* New York, NY: Dutton Children's Books/Penguin Group.

Bodovski, K., & Farkas, G. (2007). Mathematics growth in early elementary school: The roles of beginning knowledge, student engagement, and instruction. *The Elementary School Journal, 108*(2), 115–130.

Bowlby, J. (1982). *Attachment and loss: Vol. 1. Attachment.* New York, NY: Basic Books. (Original work published 1969)

Bowlby, J. (1988). *A secure base: Parent-child attachment and healthy human development.* London, England: Perseus Books.

Boykin, A. W. (1983). The academic performance of Afro-American children. In J. Spence (Ed.), *Achievement and achievement motives* (pp. 321–371). San Francisco, CA: Freeman.

Boykin, A. W. (1994). Afrocultural expression and its implications for schooling. In E. R. Hollins, J. E. King, & W. C. Hayman (Eds.), *Teaching diverse populations: Formulating a knowledge base* (pp. 225–273). Albany: State University of New York Press.

Boykin, A. W. (2001). The challenges of cultural socialization in the schooling of African American elementary school children: Exposing the hidden curriculum. In W. Watkins, J. Lewis, & V. Chou (Eds.), *Race and education: The roles of history and society in educating African American students* (pp. 190–199). Newton, MA: Allyn & Bacon.

Boykin, A. W. (2013). On enhancing academic outcomes for African American children and youth. In *Being Black is not a risk factor: A strengths-based look at the state of the Black child* (pp. 28–31). Washington, DC: National Black Child Development Institute.

Boykin, A. W., Albury, A., Tyler, K. M., Hurley, E. A., Bailey, C. T., & Miller, O. A. (2005). Culture-based perceptions of academic achievement among low-income elementary students. *Cultural Diversity and Ethnic Minority Psychology, 11*(4), 339–350.

Boykin, A. W., & Bailey, C. (2000). *The role of cultural factors in school relevant cognitive functioning: Synthesis of findings on cultural contexts, cultural orientations, and individual differences* (Report No. 42). Washington, DC, & Baltimore, MD: Howard University and Johns Hopkins University, Center for Research on the Education of Students Placed At Risk (CRESPAR).

Boykin, A. W., & Noguera, P. (2011). *Creating the opportunity to learn: Moving from research to practice to close the achievement gap.* Alexandria, VA: ASCD.

Brantlinger, E. (2003). *Dividing classes: How the middle class negotiates and rationalizes school advantage.* New York, NY: RoutledgeFalmer.

Brooks, J. G. (2011). *Big science for growing minds: Constructivist classrooms for young thinkers.* New York, NY: Teachers College Press.

Bryan, N. (2017). White teachers' role in sustaining the school-to-prison pipeline: Recommendations for teacher education. *The Urban Review, 49*(2), 326–345.

Bump, P. (2014, March 10). People—including cops—see Black kids as less innocent and less young than White kids. *The Atlantic.* Retrieved from www.theatlantic .com/politics/archive/2014/03/people-including-cops-view-black-kids-less -innocent-and-less-young-white-kids/359026/

Cabrera, N. J. (2013). Minority children and their families: A positive look. In *Being Black is not a risk factor: A strengths-based look at the state of the Black child* (pp. 4–7). Washington, DC: National Black Child Development Institute.

Caldwell, C. H., Kohn-Wood, L. P., Schmeelk-Cone, K. H., Chavous, T. M., & Zimmerman, M. A. (2004). Racial discrimination and racial identity as risk or protective factors for violent behaviors in African American young adults. *American Journal of Community Psychology, 33,* 91–107.

Capezzuto, S. M., & Da Ros-Voseles, D. A. (2001). Using experts to enhance classroom projects. *Young Children, 56*(2), 84–85.

Children's Defense Fund. (2007). *America's cradle to prison pipeline report.* Retrieved from www.childrensdefense.org/library/data/cradle-prison-pipeline -report-2007-full-lowres.pdf

Cole, J. M., & Boykin, A. W. (2008). Examining culturally structured learning environments with different types of music-linked movement opportunity. *Journal of Black Psychology, 34*(3), pp. 331–355.

Collier, D., & Bush, V. L. (2012). Who am I? I am who you say I am: Black male identity and teacher perceptions. In T. E. Dancy, II, & M. C. Brown, II. (Eds.). *African American males and education: Researching the convergence of race and identity* (pp. 75–100). Charlotte, NC: Information Age Publishing.

Cooney, T. M., Escalada, L. T., & Unruh, R. D. (2008). *Physics resources and instructional strategies for motivating students (PRISMS) PLUS.* Cedar Falls: University of Northern Iowa.

Cooperative Children's Book Center. (n.d.). Publishing statistics on children's books about people of color and First/Native Nations and by people of color and First/Native Nations authors and illustrations. Retrieved from ccbc.education.wisc.edu/books/pcstats.asp

Counsell, S. L. (2007). What happens when veteran and beginner teachers' life histories intersect with high-stakes testing and what does it mean for learners and teaching practice: The making of a culture of fear. *Dissertation Abstracts International, 69*(08), 325. (UMI No. 3298305)

Counsell, S. L. (2009). Abandoning the least restrictive environment in favor of natural settings: The achievement of social justice for all—it's a right not a privilege! *The Constructivist, 20*(1), 1–30.

Counsell, S. L. (2011). Becoming "science experi-mentors": Tenets of quality professional development and how they can reinvent early science learning experiences. *Science and Children, 49*(2), 52–56.

Counsell, S. L. (2017a, May). Challenging a view of children with merit and deficit assumptions in favor of a view that celebrates identity, voice, and agency. In G. Ressler (Chair), *Poverty, refugees and immigration: International stories and struggles*. Symposium conducted at the meeting of the World Forum on Early Care and Education, Auckland, New Zealand.

Counsell, S. L. (2017b). Promoting STEM with the full range of learners: Using ramps and pathways. *Exchange, 39*(3), 80–82.

Counsell, S. L., & Agran, M. (2013). Understanding the Special Olympics debate from lifeworld and systems perspectives: Moving beyond the liberal egalitarian view toward empowered recreational living. *Journal of Disability Policy Studies, 23*(4), 245–256.

Counsell, S. L., & Boody, R. M. (2013). Social pedagogy and liberal egalitarian compensatory programs: The case of Head Start. *Education Policy Analysis Archives, 21*(39). Retrieved from epaa.asu.edu/ojs/article/view/1299

Counsell, S. L., Escalada, L., Geiken, R., Sander, M., Uhlenberg, J., Van Meeteren, B., Yoshizawa, S., &. Zan, B. (2016). *STEM learning with young children: Inquiry teaching with ramps and pathways*. New York, NY: Teachers College Press.

Counsell, S. L., King, E., & Wright, J. (2013, April). *Reggio, project approach, and activity-based intervention: Child-centered learning for everyone*. Paper session presented at the spring conference of the Memphis Association for the Education of Young Children (MAEYC), Memphis, TN.

Counsell, S. L., Peat, F., Vaughan, R., & Johnson, T. (2015). Inventing mystery machines! Collaborating to improve STEM teacher preparation. *Science & Children, 52*(7), 64–70.

Counsell, S. L., Peat, F., Vaughan, R., & Johnson, T. (2016). Inventing mystery machines! Collaborating to improve STEM teacher preparation. In L. Froschauer (Ed.), *Bringing STEM to the elementary classroom* (pp. 115–122). Arlington, VA: National Science Teachers Association Press.

Counsell, S., & Sander, M. (2016). Using ramps in diverse learning communities. In S. Counsell, L. Escalada, R. Geiken, M. Sander, J. Uhlenberg, B. Van Meeteren, S. Yoshizawa & B. Zan, *STEM learning with young children: Inquiry teaching with ramps and pathways* (pp. 87–109). New York, NY: Teachers College Press.

Counsell, S., Uhlenberg, J., & Zan, B. (2013). Ramps and pathways early physical science program: Preparing educators as science mentors. In S. Koba & B. Wojnowski (Eds.), *Exemplary science: Best practices in professional development* (pp. 143–156). Arlington, VA: National Science Teachers Association Press.

Counsell, S. L., & Wright, B. L. (2016). Science learning for all young scientists: Exploring, investigating, learning, and growing with ramps and pathways in diverse settings. *Childhood Education, 92*(5), 365–372. doi:10.1080/00094056 .2016.1226110

Crumpton, H., & Gregory, A. (2011). "I'm not learning": The role of academic relevancy for low-achieving students. *Journal of Educational Research, 104*(1), 42–53.

Cunningham, C. M. (2009). Engineering is elementary. *The Bridge, 30*(3), 11–17.

Dancy T. E. (2014). The adultification of Black boys. In K. J. Fasching-Varner, R. E. Reynolds, K. A. Albert, & L. L. Martin (Eds.), *Trayvon Martin, race, and American justice. Teaching race and ethnicity* (pp. 49–55). Rotterdam, Netherlands: SensePublishers.

Dandy, E. (1991). *Black communications: Breaking down the barriers.* Chicago, IL: African American Images.

Darling-Hammond, L., & Bransford, J. (Eds.). (2005). *Preparing teachers for a changing world: What teachers should learn and be able to do.* San Francisco, CA: Jossey-Bass.

Davis, J. E. (2005). Early schooling and academic achievement of African American males. In O. S. Fashola (Ed.), *Educating African American males: Voices from the field* (pp. 129–150). Thousand Oaks, CA: Corwin Press.

Davis, M. H. (1994). *Empathy: A social psychological approach.* Boulder, CO: Westview Press.

Delpit, L. (1995). *Other people's children: Cultural conflict in the classroom.* New York, NY: New Press.

Delpit, L. (2006). *Other people's children: Cultural conflict in the classroom* (Updated ed.). New York, NY: New Press.

Delpit, L., & Dowdy J. K. (Eds.). (2002). *The skin that we speak: Thoughts on language and culture in the classroom.* New York, NY: New Press.

Derman-Sparks, L. (2008). Why an anti-bias curriculum. In A. Pelo (Ed.), *Rethinking early childhood education* (pp. 7–16). Milwaukee, WI: Rethinking Schools.

Derman-Sparks, L., & the A.B.C. Task Force. (1989). *Anti-bias curriculum tools for empowering young children.* Washington, DC: National Association for the Education of Young Children.

Derman-Sparks, L., & Edwards, J. O. (2010). *Anti-bias education for young children and ourselves.* Washington, DC: National Association for the Education of Young Children.

Developmental Studies Center. (1996). *Ways we want our class to be: Class meetings that build commitment to kindness and learning.* Oakland, CA: Author.

DeVries, R., Haney, J., & Zan, B. (1991). Sociomoral atmosphere in direct-instruction, eclectic, and constructivist kindergartens: A study of teachers' enacted interpersonal understanding. *Early Childhood Research Quarterly, 6,* 449–471.

DeVries, R., & Kohlberg, L. (1987). *Constructivist early education: Overview and comparison with other programs.* Washington, DC: National Association for the Education of Young Children.

DeVries, R., & Sales, C. (2011). *Ramps & pathways: A constructivist approach to physics with young children*. Washington, DC: National Association for the Education of Young Children.

DeVries, R., & Zan, B. (2012). *Moral classrooms, moral children: Creating a constructivist atmosphere in early education* (2nd ed.). New York, NY: Teachers College Press.

DeVries, R., Zan, B., Hildebrandt, C., Edmiaston, R., & Sales, C. (2002). *Developing constructivist early childhood curriculum: Practical principles and activities*. New York, NY: Teachers College Press.

Diggs, T. (2011). *Chocolate me!* New York, NY: Square Fish/Feiwel Friends /Imprints of Macmillan.

Dobbins, D., McCready, M., & Rackas, L. (2016). *Unequal access: Barriers to early childhood education for boys of color*. Retrieved from usa.childcareaware.org /wp-content/uploads/2016/10/UnequalAccess_BoysOfColor.pdf

Dodd-Nufrio, A. T. (2011). Reggio Emilia, Maria Montessori, and John Dewey: Dispelling teachers' misconceptions and understanding theoretical foundations. *Early Childhood Education Journal, 39*(4), 235–237.

Drummond, J. B., & Bynum, B. K. (2016). *I'm a brilliant little Black boy!* Los Angeles, CA: DreamTitle.

Eisenberg, N., & Strayer, J. (Eds.). (1997). *Empathy and its development*. New York, NY: Cambridge University Press.

Emdin, C. (2012). Yes, Black males are different, but different is not deficient. *Kappan Magazine, 93*(5), 13–16.

Emdin, C. (2016). *For White folks who teach in the hood . . . and the rest of y'all too: Reality pedagogy and urban education*. Boston, MA: Beacon Press.

Epstein, R., Blake, J. J., & González, T. (2017). *Girlhood interrupted: The erasure of Black girls' childhood*. Washington, DC: Georgetown Law Center on Poverty and Inequality.

Fantuzzo, J., Coolahan, K., Mendez, J., McDermott, P., & Sutton-Smith, B. (1998). Contextually-relevant validation of peer play constructs with African American Head Start children: Penn interactive peer play scale. *Early Childhood Research Quarterly, 13*(3), 411–431.

Fergus, E., Noguera, P., & Martin, M. (2014). *Schooling for resilience: Improving the life trajectory of Black and Latino boys*. Cambridge, MA: Harvard Education Press.

Ferguson, A. (2000). *Bad boys: Public schools in the making of Black masculinity*. Ann Arbor: University of Michigan Press.

Fischer, F. (1985). Critical evaluation of public policy: A methodological case study. In J. Forester (Ed.), *Critical theory and public life* (pp. 231–257). Cambridge, MA: MIT Press.

Ford, D. Y. (2010). *Reversing underachievement among gifted Black students* (2nd ed.). Waco, TX: Prufrock Press.

Ford, D. Y. (2011). *Multicultural gifted education* (2nd ed.). Waco, TX: Prufrock Press.

Ford, D. Y. (2013). *Recruiting and retaining culturally different students in gifted education*. Waco, TX: Prufrock Press.

Ford, D. Y., & Harris, III, J. J. (1999). *Multicultural gifted education*. New York, NY: Teachers College Press.

Ford, D. Y., & Milner, H. R. (2005). *Teaching culturally diverse gifted students.* Waco, TX: Prufrock Press.

Ford, D. Y., Wright, B. L., Grantham, T. C., & Moore, III, J. L. (2017). Infusing culture and equity in gifted education for students of color: Three frameworks. In J. Plucker, A. Rinn-McCann, & M. Makel (Eds.), *Giftedness: Reflecting theory in practice* (pp. 183–201). Waco, TX: Prufrock Press.

Galindo, C., & Fuller, B. (2010). The social competence of Latino kindergartners and growth in mathematical understanding. *Developmental Psychology, 46*(3), 579.

Gandini, L. (1997). Foundations of the Reggio Emilia approach. In J. Hendricks (Ed.), *First steps toward teaching the Reggio way* (pp. 14–25). Upper Saddle River, NJ: Prentice Hall.

Gangi, J. M. (2004). *Encountering children's literature: An arts approach.* Boston, MA: Allyn & Bacon.

Gay, G. (2010). *Culturally responsive teaching: Theory, research, and practice.* New York, NY: Teachers College Press.

Geiken, R., Uhlenberg, J., & Yoshizawa, S. (2016). Implementing ramps and pathways in the classroom. In S. Counsell, L. Escalada, R. Geiken, M. Sander, J. Uhlenberg, B. Van Meeteren, . . . B. Zan, *STEM learning with young children: Inquiry teaching with ramps and pathways* (pp. 29–51). New York, NY: Teachers College Press.

Gilliam, W. S. (2005). *Prekindergartners left behind: Expulsion rates in state prekindergarten programs* (Policy Brief No. 3). New York, NY: Foundation for Child Development.

Gilliam, W. S., & Reyes, C. (2016). *Teacher decision-making factors that lead to preschool expulsion: Scale development and preliminary validation of the preschool expulsion risk measure.* Manuscript submitted for review.

Goff, P. A., Jackson, M. C., Di Leone, B. A. L., Culotta, C. M., & DiTomasso, N. A. (2014). The essence of innocence: Consequences of dehumanizing Black children. *Journal of Personality and Social Psychology, 106*(4), 526–545.

Gottlieb, G. (1997). *Synthesizing nature–nurture: Prenatal roots of instinctive behavior.* Mahwah, NJ: Erlbaum.

Gottlieb, G. (2003). On making behavioral genetics truly developmental. *Human Development, 46,* 337–355.

Gould, S.J. (1996). *The mismeasure of man.* New York, NY: W. W. Norton & Company.

Graves, S. (2008). Are we neglecting African American males: Parental involvement differences between African American males and females during elementary school? *African American Studies, 14,* 263–276.

Graves, S., & Howes, C. (2011). Ethnic differences in social–emotional development in preschool: The impact of teacher child relationships and classroom quality. *School Psychology Quarterly, 26*(3), 202–214.

Griebling, S. (2011). Discoveries from a Reggio-inspired classroom: Meeting developmental needs through the visual arts. *Art Education, 64*(2), 6–11.

Gutiérrez, K. D., & Rogoff, B. (2003). Cultural ways of learning: Individual traits or repertoires. *Educational Researcher, 32*(5), 19–25.

Habermas, J. (1987). *The theory of communicative action: Vol. 2. Lifeworld and system: A critique of functional reason* (T. McCarthy, Trans.). Boston, MA: Beacon Press.

Hale, J. E. (1982). *Black children: Their roots, culture, and learning styles*. Provo, UT: Brigham Young University Press.

Hallinger, P., Bickman, L., & Davis, K. (1996). School context, principal leadership, and student reading achievement. *The Elementary School Journal, 96,* 527–549.

Hammond, Z. (2015). *Culturally responsive teaching and the brain: Promoting authentic engagement and rigor among culturally and linguistically diverse students*. Thousand Oaks, CA: Corwin Press.

Harper, F. D., Terry, L. M., & Twiggs, R. (2009). Counseling strategies with Black boys and Black men: Implications for policy. *Journal of Negro Education, 78,* 216–232.

Harper, S. R. (2010). An anti-deficit achievement framework for research on students of color in STEM. *New Directions for Institutional Research, 148,* 63–74.

Harper, S. R. (2012). *Black male student success in higher education: A report from the National Black Male College Achievement Study*. Philadelphia: University of Pennsylvania, Center for the Study of Race and Equity in Education.

Harper, S. R. (2015). Success in these schools? Visual counter narratives of young men of color and urban high schools they attend. *Urban Education, 50,* 139–169. doi:10.1177/0042085915569738

Harper, S. R., & Associates. (2014). *Succeeding in the city: A report from the New York City Black and Latino male high school achievement study*. Philadelphia: Center for the Study of Race & Equity in Education, University of Pennsylvania.

Hart, B., & Risley, T. R. (1995). *Meaningful differences in the everyday experience of young American children*. Baltimore, MD: Brookes.

Hart, B., & Risley, T. R. (2011). *The early catastrophe*. Retrieved from www.aft.org/sites/default/files/periodicals/TheEarlyCatastrophe.pdf

Hart, C., Burts, D., & Charlesworth, R. (Eds.). (1997). *Integrated curriculum and developmentally appropriate practice: Birth to age eight*. Albany: State University of New York Press.

Harte, H. A. (2010). The project approach: A strategy for inclusive classrooms. *Young Exceptional Children, 13*(3), 15–28.

Heath, S. B. (1983). *Ways with words: Language, life, and work in communities and classrooms*. New York, NY: Cambridge University Press.

Helm, J. H. (2004). Projects that power young minds. *Educational Leadership, 62*(1), 58–62.

Helm, J. H., & Beneke, S. (Eds.). (2003). *The power of projects: Meeting contemporary challenges in early childhood classrooms—Strategies and solutions*. New York, NY: Teachers College Press.

Helm, J. H., & Katz, L. G. (2011). *Young investigators: The project approach in the early years* (2nd ed.). New York, NY: Teachers College Press.

Hendrick, J. (Ed.). (2004). *Next steps toward teaching the Reggio way: Accepting the challenge to change*. Upper Saddle River, NJ: Pearson.

Hmelo, C., Holton, D., & Kolodner, J. (2000). Designing to learn about complex systems. *Journal of the Learning Sciences, 9*(3), 247–298.

Holzman, M. (2006). *Public education and Black male students: The 2006 state report card*. Schott Educational Inequity Index. Cambridge, MA: The Schott Foundation for Public Education.

Hotchkins, B. (2016). African American males navigate racial microaggression. *Teachers College Record, 118*(6), 1–36.

Howard, E. F. (1991). Authentic multicultural literature for children: An author's perspective. In M. Lindgren (Ed.), *The multicolored mirror: Cultural substance in literature for children and young adults* (pp. 91–99). Fort Atkinson, WI: Highsmith Press.

Howard, T. C. (2008). Who really cares? The disenfranchisement of African American males in prek-12 schools: A critical race theory perspective. *Teachers College Record, 110,* 954–985.

Howard, T. C. (2010). *Why race and culture matter in schools: Closing the achievement gap in America's classrooms.* New York, NY: Teachers College Press.

Howard, T. C. (2014). *Black male(d): Peril and promise in the education of African American males.* New York, NY: Teachers College Press.

Howard, T. C., & Associates (2017). *The counter narrative: Reframing success of high achieving Black and Latino males in Los Angeles County.* Los Angeles: University of California, Los Angeles. UCLA Black Male Institute.

Howell, J., & Reinhard, K. (2015). *Rituals and traditions: Fostering a sense of community in preschool.* Washington, DC: National Association for the Education of Young Children.

Hudson, W. (1991). *Jamal's busy day.* East Orange, NJ: Just Us Books.

Hughes, J. N. (2011). Longitudinal effects of teacher and student perceptions of teacher–student relationship qualities on academic adjustment. *Elementary School Journal, 112*(1), 38–60.

Hughes-Hassell, S., Kumasi, K., Rawson, C. H., & Hitson, A. (2012). *Building a bridge to literacy for African American male youth: A call to action for the library community.* Retrieved from bridgetolit.web.unc.edu/files/2012/09/Building -A-Bridge-to-Literacy-for-African-American-Males.pdf

Irvine, J. J. (1990). *Black students and school failure: Policies, practices, and prescriptions.* New York, NY: Praeger.

Irving, M. A., & Hudley, C. (2008). Cultural identification and academic achievement among African American males. *Journal of Advanced Academics, 19*(4), 676–698.

Johns, D. J. (2013). Supporting educational excellence for African Americans beginning at birth. In *Being Black is not a risk factor: A strengths-based look at the state of the Black child* (pp. 54–56). Washington, DC: National Black Child Development Institute.

Johns, D. J. (2016). Expanding high-quality early care and education for Black boys. In S. R. Harper & J. L. Wood (Eds.), *Advancing Black male student success from preschool through Ph.D.* (pp. 1–19). Sterling, VA: Stylus.

Johnson, D., & Johnson, R. (2009). An educational psychology success story: Social interdependence theory and cooperative learning. *Educational Researcher, 38*(5), 365–379.

Kamii, C. (1980). Why use group games? In C. Kamii & R. DeVries (Eds.), *Group games in early education: Implications of Piaget's theory* (pp. 11–27). Washington, DC: National Association for the Education of Young Children.

Kamii, C., & DeVries, R. (1993). *Physical knowledge in preschool education: Implications of Piaget's theory.* New York, NY: Teachers College Press.

Katz, L. G., & Chard, S. C. (2000). *Engaging children's minds: The project approach* (2nd ed.). Stamford, CT: Ablex.

Kena, G., Hussar W., McFarland J., de Brey C., Musu-Gillette, L., Wang, X., Zhang, J., Rathbun, A., WilkinsonFlicker, S., Diliberti M., Barmer, A., Bullock Mann, F., and Dunlop Velez, E. (2016). *The condition of education 2016 (NCES 2016-144)*. Washington, DC: U.S. Department of Education, National Center for Education Statistics. Retrieved from nces.ed.gov/pubs2016/2016144.pdf

Kennedy, E. (1995). Contextual effects on academic norms among elementary school students. *Educational Research Quarterly, 18*, 5–13.

Kilpatrick, W. H. (1918). The project method. *Teachers College Record, 19*, 319–335.

Kinloch, V. (2012). *Crossing boundaries: Teaching and learning with urban youth.* New York, NY: Teachers College Press.

Kirkland, D. E. (2013). *A search past silence: The literacy of young Black men.* New York, NY: Teachers College Press.

Kliewer, C. (1998). The meaning of inclusion. *Mental Retardation, 36*(4), 317–322.

Knight, D. J. (2014). Toward a relational perspective on young Black and Latino males: The contextual patterns of disclosure as coping. *Harvard Educational Review, 84*, 433–467.

Kohn, A. (1999). *The schools our children deserve: Moving beyond traditional classrooms and tougher standards.* New York, NY: Houghton Mifflin.

Kohn, A. (2006). *Beyond discipline: From compliance to community* (2nd ed.). Alexandria, VA: Association for Supervision and Curriculum Development.

Ladson-Billings, G. (2009). *The dreamkeepers: Successful teachers of African American children* (2nd ed.). San Francisco, CA: Jossey-Bass.

Ladson-Billings, G. (2011). Boyz to men? Teaching to restore Black boys' childhood. *Race, Ethnicity, and Education, 14*, 7–15.

Lareau, A. (2011). *Unequal childhoods: Class, race, and family life* (2nd ed.). Berkeley & Los Angeles: University of California Press.

Larrick, N. (1965, September 11). The all-White world of children's books. *Saturday Review*, 63–65, 84–85.

Lee, C. D. (2007). *Culture, literacy, and learning: Taking bloom in the midst of the whirlwind.* New York, NY: Teachers College Press.

Lee, C. D., Spencer, M. B., & Harpalani, V. (2003). "Every shut eye ain't sleep": Studying how people live culturally. *Educational Researcher, 32*(5), 6–13.

Lewin-Benham, A. (2011). *Twelve best practices for early childhood education: Integrating Reggio and other inspired approaches.* New York, NY: Teachers College Press.

Lewis, O. (1959). *Five families: Mexican case studies in the culture of poverty.* New York, NY: Basic Books.

Li-Grining, C. P. (2012). The role of cultural factors in the development of Latino preschoolers' self-regulation. *Child Development Perspectives, 6*(3), 210–217.

LoCasale-Crouch, J., Konold, T., Pianta, R., Howes, C., Burchinal, M., Bryant, D., Clifford, R., Early, D., & Barbarin, O. (2007). Profiles of observed classroom quality in state-funded pre-kindergarten programs and associations with teacher, program, and classroom characteristics. *Early Childhood Research Quarterly, 22*(1), 3–17.

Losen, D. J. (2013). Discipline policies, successful schools, racial justice, and the law. *Family Court Review, 51,* 388–400.

Losen, D. J., & Gillespie, J. (2012). *Opportunities suspended: The disparate impact of disciplinary exclusion from school.* Los Angeles: Civil Rights Project, University of California, Los Angeles.

Lubeck, S. (1994). The politics of developmentally appropriate practice: Exploring issues of culture, class, and curriculum. In B. Mallory & R. New (Eds.), *Diversity and developmentally appropriate practices* (pp. 17–43). New York, NY: Teachers College Press.

Martalock, P. L. (2012). "What is a wheel?" The image of the child: Traditional, project approach, and Reggio Emilia perspectives. *Dimensions of Early Childhood, 40*(3), 3–11.

McFarland, J., Hussar, B., de Brey, C., Snyder, T., Wang, X., Wilkinson-Flicker, S., . . . Hinz, S. (2017). *The condition of education 2017* (NCES 2017-144). Washington, DC: U.S. Department of Education, National Center for Education Statistics. Retrieved from nces.ed.gov/pubs2017/2017144.pdf

McGee, E. O. (2015). Why do so few Black males go into STEM areas? Here's what made DeAndre give up. Retrieved from theconversation.com/why-do-so-few -black-males-go-into-stem-areas-heres-what-made-deandre-give-up-40360

McIntosh, P. (1988). *White privilege and male privilege: A personal account of coming to see correspondences through work in women's studies* (Working Paper No. 189). Wellesley, MA: Wellesley College Center for Research on Women.

McKown, C., & Weinstein, R. S. (2008). Teacher expectations, classroom context, and the achievement gap. *Journal of School Psychology, 46*(3), 235–261.

McNair, J. C. (2014). I didn't know there were Black cowboys: Introducing African American families to African American children's literature. *Young Children, 69*(1), 64–69.

Milner, H. R., IV. (2010). *Start where you are, but don't stay there: Understanding diversity, opportunity gaps, and teaching in today's classrooms.* Cambridge, MA: Harvard Education Press.

Milner, H. R., IV. (2015). *Rac(e)ing to class: Confronting poverty and race in schools and classrooms.* Cambridge, MA: Harvard Education Press.

Moore, E., Jr., Michael, A., & Penick-Parks, M. (Eds.). (2018). *The guide for White women who teach Black boys.* Thousand Oaks, CA: Corwin Press.

Morgan, P. L., Farkas, G., Hillemeier, M. M., Mattison, R., Maczuga, S., Li, H., & Cook, M. (2015). Minorities are disproportionately underrepresented in Special Education: Longitudinal evidence across five disability conditions. *Educational Researcher, 44*(5), 278–292. doi:10.3102/0013189X15591157

Morial, M. H. (2007). *The state of Black America 2007: Portrait of the Black male.* Silver Springs, MD: Beckham Publications.

Murphy, E. G., & Nesby, T. (2002). *A map for inclusion: Building cultural competency.* Pullman: Washington State University Cooperative Extension.

Naglieri, J. A., & Ford, D. Y. (2005). Increasing minority children's representation in gifted education: A response to Lohman. *Gifted Child Quarterly, 49*(1), 29–36.

Naglieri, J. A., & Ford, D. Y. (2015). Misconceptions about the Naglieri Nonverbal Ability Test: A commentary of concerns and disagreements. *Roeper Review, 37*(4), 234–240.

Nasir, N. S. (2012). *Racialized identities: Race and achievement among African American youth.* Stanford, CA: Stanford University Press.

Nasir, N., Rosebery, A., Warren, B., & Lee, C. D. (2006). Learning as a cultural process: Achieving equity through diversity. In K. Sawyer (Ed.), *The Cambridge handbook of the learning sciences.* Cambridge, MA: Cambridge University Press.

National Association for the Education of Young Children (NAEYC). (1995). *School readiness. A position statement.* Retrieved from https://www.naeyc .org/sites/default/files/globally-shared/downloads/PDFs/resources/position -statements/PSREADY98.PDF

National Association for the Education of Young Children (NAEYC). (2009). *Developmentally appropriate practice in early childhood programs serving children from birth through age 8* (Position Statement). Washington, DC: Author. Retrieved from www.naeyc.org/sites/default/files/globally-shared/downloads /PDFs/resources/position-statements/PSDAP.pdf

National Council for the Social Studies (NCSS). (2010). National curriculum standards for social studies: A framework for teaching, learning, and assessment. Silver Spring, MD: Author.

National Education Association. (2011). *Focus on Blacks. Race against time: Educating Black boys.* Retrieved from www.nea.org/assets/docs /educatingblackboys11rev.pdf

National Research Council. (2007). *Taking science to school: Learning and teaching science in grades K–8.* Washington, DC: National Academy Press.

Neuman, S. B., & Moland, N. (2016). Book deserts: The consequences of income segregation on children's access to print. *Urban Education,* 1–22. Advance online publication. doi: 10.1177/0042085916654525

Nieto, S. (Ed.). (2005). *Why we teach.* New York, NY: Teachers College Press.

Nieto, S. (2010). *The light in their eyes: Creating multicultural learning communities.* New York, NY: Teachers College Press.

Noguera, P. A. (2003). The trouble with Black boys: The role and influence of environmental and cultural factors on the academic performance of African American males. *Urban Education, 38,* 431–459.

Noguera, P. A. (2008). *The trouble with Black boys: And other reflections on race, equity, and the future of public education.* San Francisco, CA: Jossey-Bass.

Oakes, J. (1993). Tracking, inequality, and the rhetoric of reform: Why schools don't change. In H. S. Shapiro & D. E. Purpel (Eds.), *Critical social issues in American education: Toward the 21st century* (pp. 85–102). White Plains, NY: Longman.

O'Bryant, S. (2014, December 11). A racist system. *Arkansas Times.* Retrieved from www.arktimes.com/arkansas/a-racist-system/Content?oid=3575360

Palincsar, A. S., Magnusson, S. J., Collins, K. M., & Cutter, J. (2001). Making science accessible to all: Results of a design experiment in inclusive classrooms. *Learning Disability Quarterly, 24,* 15–32.

Paris, D. (2012). Culturally sustaining pedagogy: A needed change in stance, terminology, and practice. *Educational Researcher, 41*(3), 93–97. doi:10 .3102/0013189X12441244

Piaget, J. (1973). *To understand is to invent: The future of education.* New York, NY: Grossman.

Piaget, J. (1981). *Intelligence and affectivity.* Palo Alto, CA: Annual Reviews.

Powell, D. (1994). Parents, pluralism, and the NAEYC statement on developmentally appropriate practices. In B. Mallory & R. New (Eds.), *Diversity and developmentally appropriate practices* (pp. 166–182). New York, NY: Teachers College Press.

Rahman, S., Yasin, R., & Yassin, S. F. M. (2012). Project-based approach at preschool setting. *World Applied Sciences Journal, 16*(1), 106–112.

Ramsey, P. G. (2015). *Teaching and learning in a diverse world: Multicultural education for young children* (4th ed.). New York, NY: Teachers College Press.

Rashid, H. M. (2013). Significant—but not sufficient: Quality early education and the development of young African American boys. In *Being Black is not a risk factor: A strengths-based look at the state of the Black child* (pp. 28–31). Washington, DC: National Black Child Development Institute.

Rasinski, T. V. (2010). *The fluent reader: Oral and silent reading strategies for building fluency, word recognition, and comprehension* (2nd ed.). New York, NY: Scholastic.

Rasinski, T. V., & Padak, N. D. (1990). Multicultural learning through children's literature. *Language Arts, 67*, 576–580.

Ratey, J. (2002). *A user's guide to the brain: Perception, attention, and the four theaters of the brain*. New York, NY: Vintage.

Rogoff, B. (2003). *The cultural nature of human development*. New York, NY: Oxford University Press.

Rosebery, A. S., & Warren, B. (2001). Understanding diversity in science and mathematics. *Hands on! 24*(2), 1, 4–6.

Rosenthal, R., & Jacobson, L. (1968). *Pygmalion in the classroom: Teacher expectations and pupils' intellectual development*. New York, NY: Holt, Rinehart and Winston.

Ryan, A. M. (2006). The role of social foundations in preparing teachers for culturally relevant practice. *Multicultural Education, 13*(3), 10–13.

Sampson, D., & Garrison-Wade, D. F. (2011). Cultural vibrancy: Exploring the preferences of African American children toward culturally relevant and non-culturally relevant lessons. *The Urban Review, 43*(2), 279–309.

Schott Foundation for Public Education. (2012). *Yes we can: The Schott 50 state report on public education and Black males*. Cambridge, MA: Author.

Schott Foundation for Public Education. (2015). *Black lives matter: The Schott 50 State report on public education and Black males*. Cambridge, MA: Author.

Schroeder, R. (n.d.). *Strengthening STEM learning for Black students*. Retrieved from promisemagazine.org/strengthening-stem-learning-for-black-students/

Schunn, C. (2009). How kids learn engineering: The cognitive science perspective. *The Bridge: Linking Engineering and Society, 39*(3), 32–37.

Shields, P. M. (1995). Engaging children of diverse backgrounds. In M. S. Knapp (Ed.), *Teaching for meaning in high-poverty classrooms* (pp. 33–46). New York, NY: Teachers College Press.

Sleeter, C. E., & Milner, H. R. (2011). Researching successful efforts in teacher education to diversify teachers. In A. F. Ball & C. Tyson (Eds.), *Studying diversity in teacher education* (pp. 81–103). Lanham, MD: Rowman & Littlefield.

Smith, M. (2012). Social pedagogy from a Scottish perspective. *International Journal of Social Pedagogy, 1*(1), 46–55.

Sprung, B., Froschl, M., & Gropper, N. (2010). *Supporting boys' learning: Strategies for teacher practice, pre-K–grade 3*. New York, NY: Teachers College Press.

Stipek, D. (2004). Teaching practices in kindergarten and first grade: Different strokes for different folks. *Early Childhood Research Quarterly, 19*(4), 548–568.

Stipek, D., & Byler, P. (1997). Early childhood education teachers: Do they practice what they preach? *Early Childhood Research Quarterly, 12,* 305–325.

Sue, D. W., Bucceri, J. M., Lin, A. I., Nadal, K. L., & Torino, G. C. (2007). Racial microaggressions and the Asian American experience. *Cultural Diversity and Ethnic Minority Psychology, 13,* 72–81.

Sullivan, D. (2016). *Cultivating the genius of Black children: Strategies to close the achievement gap in the early years*. St. Paul, MN: Redleaf Press.

Tatum, A. W. (2005). *Teaching reading to Black adolescent males: Closing the achievement gap*. Portland, ME: Stenhouse.

Tatum, A. W. (2009). *Reading for their life: (Re)building the textual lineages of African American adolescent males*. Portsmouth, NH: Heinemann.

Thompson, G. L. (2002). *African American teens discuss their schooling experiences*. Westport, CT: Bergin & Garvey.

Thompson, M. C. (1996). Mentors on paper: How classics develop verbal ability. In J. Van Tassel-Baska, D. T. Johnson, & L. N. Boyce (Eds.), *Developing verbal talent: Ideas and strategies for teachers of elementary and middle school students* (pp. 56–74). Boston, MA: Allyn & Boston.

Todd, A. R., Thiem, K. C., & Neel, R. (2016). Does seeing faces of young Black boys facilitate the identification of threatening stimuli? *Psychological Science, 27,* 384–393. doi:101177/0956797615624492

Toldson, I. A. (2008). *Breaking barriers: Plotting the path to academic success for school-age African-American males*. Washington, DC: Congressional Black Caucus Foundation.

Toldson, I. A., & Johns, D. J. (2016). Erasing deficits. *Teachers College Record, 118*(6), 1–7.

Trotman Scott, M., Wright, B. L., & Ford, D. Y. (2018). The book matters: Using the color-coded Bloom–Banks matrix to support the literacy and engagement of Black boys. In E. Moore, Jr., A. Michael, & M. W. Penick-Parks (Eds.), *The guide for White women who teach Black boys* (pp. 356–362). Thousand Oaks, CA: Corwin Press.

Tyler, K. M., Boykin, A. W., & Walton, T. R. (2006). Cultural considerations in teachers' perceptions of student classroom behavior and achievement. *Teaching and Teacher Education, 22,* 998–1005.

Upchurch, C. (1997). *Convicted in the womb*. New York, NY: Bantam Books.

U.S. Department of Education. (2015). *A matter of equity: Preschool in America*. Retrieved from www2.ed.gov/documents/early-learning/matter-equity-preschool-america.pdf

U.S. Department of Education Office for Civil Rights. (2014). *Civil rights data collection: Snapshot: School discipline*. Retrieved from ocrdata.ed.gov/Downloads/CRDC-School-Discipline-Snapshot.pdf

U.S. Department of Education Office for Civil Rights. (2016). *2013–2014 civil rights data collection: A first look*. Retrieved from www2.ed.gov/about/offices/list/ocr/docs/2013-14-first-look.pdf

Vance, E. (2015). *Class meetings: Young children solving problems together* (Rev. ed.). Washington, DC: National Association for the Education of Young Children.

Van Meeteren, B. (2016). Ramps and pathways promote communication development. In S. Counsell, L. Escalada, R. Geiken, M. Sander, J. Uhlenberg, B. Van Meeteren, . . . B. Zan, *STEM learning with young children: Inquiry teaching with ramps and pathways* (pp. 29–51). New York, NY: Teachers College Press.

Varelas, M., Martin, D. B., & Kane, J. M. (2013). Content learning and identity construction (CLIC): A framework to strengthen African American students' mathematics and science learning in urban elementary schools. *Human Development, 55*(6), 319–339.

Vasquez, V. M. (2014). *Negotiating critical literacies with young children* (10th anniversary ed.). New York, NY: Routledge.

Waddell, L. (2010). How do we learn: African American elementary students learning reform mathematics in urban classrooms. *Journal of Urban Mathematics Education, 3*(2), 116–154.

Warren, C. A. (2013). The utility of empathy for White female teachers' culturally responsive interactions with Black male students. *Interdisciplinary Journal of Teaching and Learning, 3*(3), 175–200.

Warren, C. A. (2016). "We learn through our struggles": Nuancing notions of urban Black male academic preparation for postsecondary success. *Teachers College Record, 118*(6), 1–38.

Watkins, A. (2002). Learning styles of African American children: A developmental consideration. *Journal of Black Psychology, 28*(3), 3–17.

Webb-Johnson, G. (2002). Are schools ready for Joshua? Dimensions of African-American culture among students identified as having behavioral/emotional disorders. *Qualitative Studies in Education, 15*(6), 653–671. Retrieved from www.tandfonline.com/doi/abs/10.1080/0951839022000014367

Whiting, G. W. (2006). From at risk to at promise: Developing scholar identities among Black males. *Journal of Secondary Gifted Education, XVII*(4), 222–229.

Whiting, G. W. (2009). The Scholar Identity Institute: Guiding Darnel and other Black males. *Gifted Child Today, 32*(4), 53–56.

Wien, C. A. (Ed.). (2008). *Emergent curriculum in the primary classroom: Interpreting the Reggio Emilia approach in schools.* New York, NY: Teachers College Press.

Williams, D. D. (2015). *An RTI guide to improving the performance of African American students.* Thousand Oaks, CA: Corwin Press.

Williams, K. C., & Veomett, G. E. (2007). *Launching learners in science, preK–5: How to design standards-based experiences and engage students in classroom conversations.* Thousands Oak, CA: Corwin Press.

Wilson, A. N. (1978). *The developmental psychology of the Black child.* New York, NY: Africana Research Publications.

Wilson, R. (n.d.). Promoting the development of scientific thinking. *Early Childhood News.* Retrieved from www.earlychildhoodnews.com/earlychildhood/article_view.aspx?ArticleID=409

Woodson, G. C. (1933). *The mis-education of the Negro.* Chicago, IL: African-American Images.

Wright, B. L. (2009). Racial-ethnic identity, academic achievement, and African American males: A review of literature. *Journal of Negro Education, 78*(2), 123–134.

Wright, B. L. (2011a). I know who I am, do you? Identity and academic achievement of successful African-American male adolescents in an urban pilot high school in the U.S. *Urban Education, 46*(4), 611–638.

Wright, B. L. (Ed.). (2011b). K–16 and beyond: African American male student engagement in STEM disciplines [Special issue]. *Journal of African American Males in Education, 2*(1). Retrieved from journalofafricanamericanmales.com /issues/vol2no1

Wright, B. L. (2011c). Valuing the everyday practices of African American students K–12 and their engagement in STEM learning: A position. *Journal of Negro Education, 80*(2), 5–11.

Wright, B. L. (2016, April). It's not your thing, you can't do what you wanna do: Holding schools and society accountable for the (mis)education of African American males. *Jefferson County Public Schools, Envision Equity: Diversity, Equity and Poverty Program,* 12–13.

Wright, B. L. (2017). Five wise men: African American males using urban critical literacy to negotiate and navigate home and school in an urban setting. *Urban Education,* 1–33. Advance online publication. doi:10.1177/0042085917690203

Wright, B. L., Counsell, S. L., Goings, R. B., Freeman, H., & Peat, F. (2016). Creating access and opportunity: Preparing African American male students for STEM trajectories preK–12. *Journal for Multicultural Education, 10*(3), 384–404. doi:10.1108JME-01-2016-0003

Wright, B. L., Counsell, S. L., & Tate, S. L. (2015). We're many members, but one body: Fostering a healthy self-identity and agency in African American boys. *Young Children, 70*(3), 24–31.

Wright, B. L., Counsell, S. L., & Tate, S. L. (2016). We're many members, but one body: Fostering a healthy self-identity and agency in African American boys [With guiding questions]. In H. Bohart, H. B. Collick, & K. Charner (Eds.), *Spotlight on young children: Teaching and learning in the primary grades* (pp. 95–105). Washington, DC: National Association for the Education of Young Children.

Wright, B. L., & Ford, D. Y. (2016a). "This little light of mine": Creating positive early childhood education classroom experiences for African American boys preK–3. *Journal of African American Males in Education, 7*(1), 5–19.

Wright, B. L., & Ford, D. Y. (2016b, Spring). What are little boys made of? The vital need for equitable early childhood education classrooms for African American boys. *Living Education eMagazine, XV,* 18–17.

Wright, B. L., & Ford, D. Y. (2016c). Who is the young child? Considerations for Black males in the special education pipeline. *DDEL VOICES, 6*(1), 4–5.

Wright, B. L., & Ford, D. Y. (2017a). Multicultural pathways to STEM: Engaging young gifted Black boys using the color-coded Bloom–Banks matrix. *Gifted Child Today, 40*(4), 212–217. doi:10.1177/1076217517722577

Wright, B. L., & Ford, D. Y. (2017b). Untapped potential: Recognition of gifted in early childhood and what professionals need to know about students of color. *Gifted Child Today, 40*(2), 111–116. doi:10.1177/1076217517690862

Wright, B. L., Ford, D. Y., & Grantham, T. C. (2018). Black faces and White spaces: Recognizing and supporting Black boys in gifted education. In E. Moore, Jr., A. Michael, & M. W. Penick-Parks (Eds.), *The guide for White women who teach Black boys* (pp. 350–355). Thousand Oaks, CA: Corwin Press.

Wright, B. L., Ford, D. Y., & Walters, N. M. (2016). Karl is ready! Why aren't you? Promoting social and cultural skills in early childhood education. *Wisconsin English Journal, 58*(2), 81–101.

Wright, B. L., Ford, D. Y., & Young, J. L. (2017). Ignorance or indifference? Seeking excellence and equity for under-represented students of color in gifted education. *Global Education Review, 4*(1). 45–60.

Wright, B. L., Young, J. L., & Ford, D. Y. (2017). Will every child count? Exploring what early childhood and gifted children of color risk losing under a Trump administration. In D. T. Harris (Ed.), *Newschaser: The rhetoric of Trump in essays and commentaries* (pp. 133–146). New York, NY: Universal Write Publications.

Wurm, J. P. (2005). *Working in the Reggio way: A beginner's guide for American teachers*. St. Paul, MN: Redleaf Press.

York, S. (2016). *Roots and wings: Affirming culture and preventing bias in early childhood* (3rd ed.). St. Paul, MN: Redleaf Press.

Yosso, T. J. (2005). Whose culture has capital? A critical race theory discussion of community cultural wealth. *Race Ethnicity and Education, 8*(1), 69–91.

Zan, B., & Geiken, R. (2010). Ramps and Pathways: Developmentally appropriate, intellectually rigorous, and fun physical science. *Young Children, 65*(1), 12–17.

Index

The letters *f* and *p* following a page number refer to a figure or a photo, respectively.

About the Authors

Brian L. Wright, PhD, is an assistant professor of early childhood education in the Department of Instruction and Curriculum Leadership in the College of Education at the University of Memphis, where he teaches undergraduate- and graduate-level (master's/doctoral) courses. His research examines high-achieving African American boys/males in urban schools (pre-K–12), racial-ethnic identity development of boys and young men of color, STEM and African American males, African American males as early childhood teachers, and teacher identity development. Dr. Wright has published articles in *Urban Education, Theory Into Practice*, and *The Journal of Negro Education*, to name a few. He has coauthored articles that have appeared in *Young Children, Childhood Explorer, Gifted Child Today, Handbook on Gifted Education, Psychology Forum, Journal of African American Males in Education*, and others. He is an NAEYC consulting editor and the organizer/co-leader of a special-interest forum titled Educating Black Boys and Adolescent Males, which is facilitated by the Association for Childhood Education International (www.acei.org/community/). He has given several keynote addresses and presented his research at local, state, and national conferences.

Shelly L. Counsell, EdD, is program coordinator and assistant professor of early childhood education at the University of Memphis, teaching undergraduate and graduate ECE courses. She studied constructivism and Piaget readings with Rheta DeVries. A former R&P site facilitator and research fellow at the UNI Regents' Center, Dr. Counsell is an author of *STEM Learning with Young Children: Inquiry Teaching with Ramps and Pathways*. She also has authored chapters in NSTA's *Exemplary Science PD* and *Bringing STEM to the Elementary Classroom*, and coauthored a chapter in *Spotlight on Young Children: Teaching and Learning in the Primary Grades*. A consulting editor for NAEYC's *Young Children* and book acquisitions, Dr. Counsell has published articles in *Science & Children, Young Children, Childhood Education,* and *Connected Science Learning.* She has made national and international research presentations on various topics, including constructivism, STEM, inclusion, equity, diversity, reflective practice, democratic learning communities, and high-stakes testing.